LABOUR
SHOWS THE WAY
General Editor: Clement R. Attlee, M.P.

LABOUR'S WAY
TO PEACE

by

ARTHUR HENDERSON, M.P.

1935

METHUEN & CO. LTD. LONDON

First published in 1935

PREFACE

' LABOUR'S WAY TO PEACE ' is a serious attempt to interpret with directness and clarity the official policy of organized Labour, industrial and political, in the realm of foreign affairs, rather than an expression of the personal views of the author.

The principles of Labour's foreign policy have not varied since the world war ; they have stood the test of time, and have proved both true and fruitful. But the principles have been re-stated and re-applied from time to time in the light of the changing and developing world situation. Two important considerations may be advanced in favour of a fuller re-statement of Labour's foreign policy at this juncture, and especially with regard to Peace and War : (1) the gravity of the international situation and the increasing talk of war, and (2) the fact that the Labour Party is the official Opposition and the obvious alternative to the National Government, and hopes soon to secure a majority with which to control the destinies of the nation.

Moreover, Labour believes that no aspect of the nation's responsibility requires a clearer understanding, more care and greater attention, than does the vast field of international relations.

Labour's Way to Peace states the problem and defines the methods, constructive and positive, whereby a Labour Government—given a majority —would seek to attain to a permanent peace.

A. H.

Transport House,
    Smith Square, S.W.1.
January, 1935.

CONTENTS

Section I

THE WORLD SITUATION

Section II

LABOUR'S POLICY

Section III

LABOUR'S NEW LEAD

Section I

THE WORLD SITUATION

CHAPTER I

THE CHANGING WORLD—ECONOMIC
CHANGES

T HE magnitude and complexity of the task
which must be undertaken if we are
successfully to travel *Labour's Way to Peace*
may be the more easily appreciated by a review
of the world situation during the post-war
period.

That the last two decades have witnessed
tremendous changes in the relationships of nations
cannot be challenged. In this brief time international society has been shaken to its foundations, and such drastic changes have been made
as to amount to a veritable revolution. So
complete has been the transformation of thought
and outlook, that we are now confronted with
the demand for new standards, new tests and
new purposes. An international spirit is developing—slowly it may be—and an international
society of nations has already emerged from the
pre-war conditions of anarchy and confusion.
The interdependence of nations is a fact.
Governments and peoples are beginning to
realize that their contacts with other peoples
are so continuous, so widespread, so vital, that
vast common interests of an international and

fundamental character can only be effectively promoted and maintained by joint co-operative action.

Some one recently coined the terrible phrase that since 1931 the world has passed from a post-war to a new pre-war period. Superficially indeed the world appears to be returning to pre-war : there is a new race in armaments, the fear of war is once more poisoning public life, militant nationalism has revived with a vengeance, there is a return to the belief that the way to secure peace is to prepare for war, and a groping back to the old policies—armed isolation or rival alliances—of the Balance of Power.

But a closer view shows that the world is not only in reaction, but also and above all in transition. Both economically and politically, the world is, for good or for ill, but indubitably and irrevocably, profoundly different from the world of 1914 and rapidly becoming more different.

The post-war period has witnessed an economic slump on a wider and much more protracted scale than the world has ever known. Amidst the disastrous consequences arising out of such a serious economic crisis, we are without any positive policies to guide the actions of the great majority of the world's governments. In past ages mankind has been impoverished by pestilence, famine and war, but we are living in an age of plenty and it cannot, therefore, be said that the world is suffering because the world is poor. Industry and agriculture are now equipped for production on a scale hitherto unknown, and the resources of modern transport are adequate for the swift distribution of a greater volume of material wealth if the means of making effective the demands of consumers could be found. Yet this fact has not dawned upon those in authority— or if it has they have not the necessary courage to tackle the problem from the standpoint of increasing consumption. The policy that has hitherto held the field is that of restricting production, and increasing and developing monopolist organizations, national cartels and trusts. The entire economic system of the world is thus being brought within the domination of increasingly powerful combines. Under the pressure of private interests, barriers are being placed in the way of international trade, and measures adopted for ' protection ' of markets which have the effect of limiting consumption. Under the policy at present pursued, the volume, as well as the value, of international trade have been declining steadily, and both economic and political nationalism have increased dangerously. We have witnessed a catastrophic fall in prices, the failure of the Gold Standard system, unbalanced and unplanned production and uncontrolled rationalization of industry, the impeding of trade, the cessation of international lending, the breakdown of confidence—which has spread to investors and producers of every kind—and doubts and fears about the political stability of Europe and the Far East. Governments are now compelled, in one way or another, to intervene in almost every aspect of the economic life of nations. The regulation, the conscious control, of economic forces, is a universally accepted policy, the necessity for which no one any longer disputes.

In retrospect the great slump appears as the Waterloo of the economics of individualism. Private profit-making enterprise first brought on the depression, and then in desperate attempts at self-preservation, helped to convert it into a world peace crisis and fastened on the world the nationalist reaction and the hybrid economic system under which it groans to-day. Part of the point is put very clearly by Sir Arthur Salter :

' The clue to the maze of intricate problems through which we have to find our way is to be found in the fact that we are now in a stage intermediate between these two systems—the self-regulating, automatic system in which supply adjusted itself to demand under the stimulus of competitive gain, with the guidance of changing prices, and the system under which future needs are estimated, production is directed and controlled, and distribution is organized. . . . We have, in our present intermediate position between these two systems, lost many of the advantages of both and failed to obtain the full benefits of either. Without securing the advantages of deliberate planning, we have enough official control and private privilege and monopoly to impede the automatic adjustments, and to restrict the benefits of competition to the consumer.

From this worst of both worlds we must certainly escape.'[1]

The experience hitherto of the countries that have gone in for economic planning on the basis of the private profit-seeking motive suggests that such planning is illusory and unstable. It leaves little doubt that such planning takes the form of the State yielding to the competitive importunities of organized private interests, which in their blind scramble for profits quite literally and plainly push the governments into planning on a nationalist basis for the creation of scarcity, the perpetuation of privilege and the preparation of war. That is what is actually happening before our eyes to-day, in one country after another, including our own.

The Socialist contention is that the only way to plan on a world scale for abundance, equality and peace is to substitute the common good for private profit as the basic motive in economic planning.

Labour is convinced that within the capitalist economy the dislocation between production and consumption cannot be set right by such measures as governments, in pursuit of a policy of economic nationalism, are willing to consider, for Labour believes that the capitalist system is responsible for the crisis and is powerless to provide effective remedies. It recognizes that the evils of the capitalist economic system which result in new crises at intervals, the instability of world peace, the attacks of Fascism, and other political

[1] *Recovery*, pp. 14 and 15.

disturbances, are the principal causes of the present crisis. It sees in the development of large syndicates, combines, and trusts, which are completely transforming individual enterprise, not only an acceptance of the need for unified organization, but an admission that large-scale organization is neither inherently dangerous nor impracticable. At the same time, however, Labour regards this development in capitalism as lending greater strength and urgency to its proposal that national ownership and public control should supersede capitalist ownership and private control in all industries and services which are essential to the economic security and social well-being of the nation as a whole. Labour is determined to use its opportunities for utilizing the machinery of State and all the international institutions which are available for the realization of co-operation and Socialism, by which alone can the international economic system be in a permanently healthy condition.

CHAPTER II

POLITICAL AND MILITARY CHANGES

IN the political field the changes that have occurred merely confirm the impression resulting from the preceding description of economic change. Indeed, the two are connected and the political situation is little more than the reflection of the economic forces just indicated. The characteristic feature of the situation to-day is that economic and social questions have ceased to be private affairs and have become matters concerning the whole community, whereas, conversely, most political issues to-day arise out of economic and social problems.

The second characteristic of the post-war world is the spread of nationalism. The initial impulse given by the French Revolution in the eighteenth century spread to Central Europe and subsequently to the Balkans in the nineteenth and early twentieth centuries. Everywhere the rise of nationalism was also a movement of social liberation and brought new classes to power. The world war has continued this process throughout East Europe, Russia and the Near, Middle and Far East. Africa, it is already clear, will not for ever be immune, for the sentiment of

B

nationalism knows no boundaries of race or clime.

The other changes in the world are generally due, directly or indirectly, to the two primary factors mentioned. In Europe a series of new national States and régimes have emerged. Most of these are militantly nationalist in character, and are attempting some form of Fascist or quasi-Fascist social reorganization. But the change likely to have the greatest effect on the future of humanity is the conversion of the Empire of the Tsars into the Union of Socialist Soviet Republics, a Communist association of States stretching from the Arctic Ocean to the Black Sea and from the Baltic to the Pacific, proclaiming as its ultimate object world union on the basis of Socialism, and now occupying a position in the League of Nations and its Council as a first-class great power.

The world's political centre of gravity is shifting from Europe to the Far East. This is partly because of the increasing importance, both relatively and absolutely, of Asia and America in the world's trade and industry. Partly because of the spread of nationalism throughout the East and particularly in China. Partly because of the gigantic social and economic experiment in the United States, and because that country now has naval parity with Great Britain and is concentrating her fleet in the Pacific. Partly because of Japan's bid for world power, hegemony in the Far East and commercial supremacy.

Since the war the British Empire has evolved into the British Commonwealth of Nations—a unique and unprecedented community, comprising wellnigh every race and language, every form of political rule and relationship, scattered over the seven seas and the five continents, covering one-quarter of the earth and one-fifth of its inhabitants, and ranging from insignificant coaling stations to the stately Indian Empire and the great Dominions, who are independent States in all but name, and among whom Great Britain occupies only the position of first among equals. The evolution of the Dominions into a co-equal and independent status, the workings of nationalism in India and Egypt, the loss of British commercial and industrial supremacy, the acceptance of naval parity with the United States, the rise of the air arm, the institution of the mandates system and the separate League membership of the United Kingdom, the Irish Free State, the Dominions and India—these things have transformed the position of Great Britain in the world and make any return to pre-war conditions impossible.

Three facts stand out in considering Great Britain's position in the post-war world. The first is that we have nothing to gain and every-thing to lose by war. Apart from the question of a better distribution of existing wealth, economic recovery in this country cannot advance much above its present level nor be made secure against a fresh slump except by a revival of world trade. In present circumstances that means a lessening of economic nationalism and the growth of international arrangements for the planned exchange of goods. Such developments are possible only against a background of assured peace.

The second fact is that Great Britain no longer directs the British Empire autocratically, but is in the position of first among equals in the British Commonwealth of Nations, the members of which are bound by a complex variety of links to each other, to the other parts of the Empire, and to the rest of the world.

The third fact is that the British Commonwealth as a whole stands in much the same relation to the world to-day as the United Kingdom did to Europe after the Napoleonic wars. We were then a balancing and mediatory power; to-day the British Commonwealth is a connecting link between Europe, Asia, America and Africa. We are bound up with the destiny of each and can play the part of conciliator and mediator, because we share the life of all.

Successive Imperial Conferences have made it clear that it is only through common membership of the League of Nations that we can solve the problem of a common aim in foreign policy and of combining co-operation within the Commonwealth with the independence and equality of status of its members. The League could not exist without the British Commonwealth. But neither could the Commonwealth in anything like its present form survive in a world that had reverted to the Balance of Power.

These views find striking confirmation in the report of the unofficial Empire Conference at

Toronto in September, 1933, which was remarkably successful in making a cross-section of every shade of opinion in Great Britain and the Dominions. 'There was in 1933,' says the report,[1] 'a striking consensus of opinion—not only in Canada but in other British countries, including the United Kingdom—as to the intimacy of the connexion, in the post-war world, between the British Commonwealth and the Collective System of International Relations.' The preservation of peace, it was unanimously agreed, was the one common aim of Commonwealth foreign policy. 'There was unanimity in the Conference that the peoples of the Commonwealth not only desired peace, but also wished to give their fullest support to the Collective System, established since the close of the World War for this purpose. . . .'[2]

The greatest and most fundamental change in the post-war world, the change that sums up and forms the background to the others, is the founding of the League of Nations and its International Labour Organization. The fundamental idea of the latter is that world peace cannot be stable unless based on social justice. The fundamental idea of the League is that war is a crime, the commission of which in any part of the world is a matter of concern to the whole world. To give effect to this conception the members of the League have signed the most solemn treaty obligations to submit their

[1] British Commonwealth Relations, pp. 42-3.

[2] British Commonwealth Relations, p. 170.

disputes to pacific precedure, to respect and to preserve against external aggression each other's territorial integrity and political independence, to refrain from war, and to take joint action against any country that resorted to violence in defiance of these pledges. The framers of the Covenant went as far as they could at the time. They made revolutionary inroads on pre-war conceptions of sovereignty. But they could not rule out war altogether. They left a small loophole for war—the famous ' gap ' in Article 15, paragraph 7 of the Covenant. At the same time they left all the material for stopping the gap at a later date.[1]

For the Covenant was framed, with great wisdom, in such a way as to allow plenty of elasticity and room for growth. It was intended, not as the last word, but as a starting-point that was to give a new impulse and direction to the development of international relations and to induce nations to draw closer and closer together, both for co-operation on matters of common concern and for keeping the peace.

In the decade and a half that have passed since the League came into existence it has been subjected to many violent and unforeseen stresses. Many of the assumptions on which the framers of the Covenant proceeded—that capitalist democracy and economic individualism would continue to prevail in the world, that all nations would be in the League, that the cult of war was dead—have been falsified. Since the

[1] See Appendix I.

economic depression a powerful offensive has developed against not only the League but the whole conception of co-operation for peace.

Nevertheless the League has not only survived but shown remarkable powers of adaptation and growth. The experience of two Labour Governments has shown that it can be used as a powerful instrument of peace. It has lately gained a notable accession of strength through the membership of the Soviet Union. On the principle that the best defence is to attack, a Socialist counter-offensive to the nationalist reaction is developing. Its objective is nothing less than the establishment of a World Commonwealth.

The obligation to reduce and limit armaments and to grapple with the evil of private manufacture of arms and munitions of war was put in the forefront of the peace-keeping system of the Covenant, for it was recognized at the Peace Conference that the success and ultimately the survival of the League were bound up with putting national armaments under international control, at progressively lower levels and on the basis of pooled security. This problem was made more urgent by the disarmament of the Central Powers and the promise that this was a preliminary to general disarmament. Ever since the armistice, therefore, the world has been haunted by the problem of disarmament. Strenuous efforts were made at Versailles to secure immediate all-round disarmament, the obligation to disarm was inserted in the Covenant, and the League has from the first day it came into existence regarded disarmament as a primary duty. This duty has been rendered only more urgent and more grave by the tremendous increase in killing-power since the world war. The armaments of to-day are incomparably more destructive and deadly than the armaments of 1918. Armies and navies are better equipped for slaughter and ruin than ever before. The manufacture of poison gas and preparations for bacterial warfare are making great strides. A new and terrible weapon —the air arm—has developed to the point where experts declare there is no defence, but only reprisals, where attack will take the form of dropping tons of incendiary, poison gas, and bacterial bombs, and where the ' front ' will be the whole surface of the country, and particularly the densest centres of population, the great cities where beats the heart of civilization. The object of all attacks will be to still that heart, to murder civilization, and in this both sides are only too likely to prove successful.

That is the great modern paradox, the most urgent and terrible of all problems in public life. On the one hand, a Disarmament Conference actually in being, a comprehensive system of international obligations and a passionate longing for peace, and on the other, a piling up of the forces of violence and destruction in a new arms race. That paradox faces mankind with a fateful choice.

To-day the militarists are in a small minority. There are millions who are passionately convinced that Mr. Baldwin was right when he said that another war would bring down European civilization with as great a shock as that of Rome. They are ready to do anything to avoid that dread consummation, but they feel themselves caught up by a relentless destiny, involved in a vicious circle which is slowly and inexorably revolving to our doom. They see that in the name of national defence we are taking part in a new arms race and they know how that is bound to end. But they believe that unilateral disarmament would merely hasten the catastrophe they wish to avoid and so feel that they cannot deny the claim of national defence. And, indeed, on the purely national plane there is no escape from this tragic dilemma—an arms race or unilateral disarmament. The only way out is through *international* action.

The whole issue turns on what is meant by national defence. In this, as in other countries, defence is popularly spoken of as though it were a question of measures to ward off an enemy attempting to land on our soil. But not since William the Conqueror has Great Britain ever fought a war because her territory was invaded. The same is the case with the United States throughout her history. The truth is that States go to war to uphold their view of their rights and interests against some other country which is similarly determined to defend *its* view of its rights and interests. In the case of Great Britain the interest we have defended and for which we have shed oceans of blood has generally, in the last analysis, been the Balance of Power.

It took four years of world war, ten million dead, and twenty million wounded to teach statesmen and public opinion that this method of defence must be abandoned. They embodied the lesson in the Covenant.

Under the Covenant self-defence has become a matter of collective concern : the individual members of the League have given up the anarchic right of self-judged self-defence and accepted the view that it is the duty of the community of nations to decide between what is aggression and what is defence. In return for this the community of nations has accepted the duty of protecting what it decides to be a law-abiding nation engaged in self-defence against what it decides to be a law-breaker committing aggression. The methods for the peaceful settlement of disputes in the Covenant serve the double purpose of an alternative to war for settling differences and of criteria by which the community of nations can be assisted in distinguishing defence from aggression in any given case.

In the course of a decade and a half of the League's history much has been done to develop, clarify and strengthen the League's peace-keeping system. As will be shown in the next chapter the first two Labour Governments have played an honourable and leading part in this work. But since September, 1931, the world has relapsed, and to-day how to stop the new arms race is the most urgent problem of statesmanship.

Even before the war the traditional standards and methods of statecraft and the traditional concepts of patriotism and economic life out of which they arose, proved inadequate, for they were unable to avert the world war. To attempt to revert to pre-war ways to-day is suicidal folly. Yet that folly is being committed under our eyes. The forces of reaction—sometimes under cover of lip service to the League and democracy—are mobilizing under the banner of nationalism to perpetuate economic privilege and armed sovereignty, although their inevitable concomitants are poverty, tyranny and war.

That is why those who respond to the needs of the new age are rallying to the banner of Socialism as the only political faith and the only force in public life strong enough to win the battle against Fascism and war, and to lead mankind out of the Valley of the Shadow of Death into a new era of freedom, plenty and peace.

Section II

LABOUR'S POLICY

CHAPTER III

LABOUR'S RECORD AND ATTITUDE

LABOUR is essentially international in its outlook and its interests, for it has its roots in the fundamental beliefs and ideals of world Socialism. Its foreign policy is based upon the needs and convictions of the mass of ordinary men and women, for whom, as the world war and the peace have shown, foreign policy is a matter of life and death. It fully believes in the international solidarity of peoples, and, therefore, that one nation's loss is every nation's loss, and that one nation's gain is every nation's gain. The Labour Party's foreign policy springs directly from this belief. It is a policy of co-operation with all other nations and in every sphere of the common lives of the peoples of the world.

The world of to-day has inherited a legacy of war problems, intensified and complicated by vacillation on the one hand and the violation of the principles of international justice and co-operation on the other. The seats of possible strife to-day are as numerous as ever they were before the war. The times demand a new policy capable of extricating the world from the fetters forged in the name of statesmanship. Labour's policy of peace and internationalism provides the weapon by which mankind can strike off the shackles which bind it. The alternative to Labour's policy is the continuance of fear and factions, of hatred and hostility, of competition and chaos. Labour challenges, therefore, the old order, the old ways, and the old methods.

The Labour and Socialist Movement has contributed powerfully to certain features of the post-war world. The idea of a League of Nations was first taken up in Socialist circles and the writings of Socialist thinkers influenced the framers of the Covenant. The organized pressure of the Labour and Socialist Parties and the desire to make concessions to the workers had much to do with the bringing into existence of the League of Nations and the International Labour Organization.

In the first few years after the war the Labour and Socialist Parties, which had fought manfully for a reasonable and conciliatory peace settlement, were the first and strongest critics of the folly of reparations, and throughout stood for a policy which, if it had been followed, would have saved the world much needless suffering.

The first Labour Government—in a minority as it was and brief as was its tenure of office— gave an impetus to the organization of peace by the conclusion of the Geneva Protocol. In this document a realistic and intelligent attempt was made, in conjunction with the Radical-Socialist and Socialist cartel Government in France, to supply the basis of security and arbitration without which it was even then realized that disarmament was impossible.

It is too often forgotten that the Geneva Protocol was to come into force only if and when a Disarmament Convention was actually being applied, and that, as its name implies, it did nothing but implement the principles of the Covenant. The date of the Disarmament Conference was fixed, and, if the Labour Government had remained longer in office, there is small doubt that this Conference, comprising both members and non-members of the League, would have been held in 1925 on a basis of guaranteed security and in a political atmosphere which would have ensured its success. This, in turn, would have made the whole course of post-war history different, and would almost certainly have spared the world the events in the Far East and Germany which have raised the spectre of another world war.

But public opinion was unprepared. The Protocol was vigorously attacked in Great Britain in Liberal and Conservative quarters on grounds which really constituted a denial of the fundamental principles of the Covenant, and showed that the great mass of public opinion, including politicians and the Press, was still profoundly ignorant of the meaning and implications of the collective peace system, and still retained an instinctive belief that the policies of international anarchy were possible and desirable.

Nevertheless, the momentum of the forces released by the negotiation of the Protocol was sufficient to bring about the conclusion of Locarno and Germany's entry into the League. The

c

Protocol was a general arrangement, including all-in arbitration, which provided for the conclusion of regional agreements and interpreted Article 16 of the Covenant to mean the obligation to co-operate loyally and effectively in resistance to acts of aggression in so far as the geographical position and the armaments of the countries concerned allowed. The Locarno Treaties accepted this interpretation of Article 16 and were put forward as a regional agreement which should be followed by other similar agreements on the basis of the general obligations of the Covenant.

All attempts, however, to secure acceptance for the principle of arbitration were persistently refused by the Conservative Government between 1924 and 1929. In the meanwhile, the Labour Party was conducting propaganda for arbitration and notably for accession to the Optional Clause conferring compulsory jurisdiction on the Permanent Court.[1] The technical problems arising in this connexion were worked out by the competent organs of the Party.

Accordingly, when the second Labour Government came in, public opinion was prepared, and Great Britain found it possible to lead the world in accepting the Optional Clause and the General Act of Arbitration.[1] At the same time, preparations for disarmament were once more taken in hand vigorously. The Treaty for Strengthening the Means to Prevent War[2] and the Treaty for

[1] See Appendix II.

[2] See Appendix III.

Financial Assistance[1] were opened for signature with a proviso that they should come into force, so far as this country was concerned, only in connexion with a Disarmament Convention, and the amendment of the Covenant was proposed so as to make it renounce war completely in conformity with the Kellogg-Briand Pact.[2]

Even as far back as 1924, when the Protocol was concluded, the British, French, and other Governments had announced that in the conditions created by the coming into force of this agreement, together with a Disarmament Convention, it would be possible and desirable to take up the question on the one hand of facilitating peaceful change and on the other of far-reaching policies of economic co-operation. The second Labour Government, in addition to pressing on with the measures described, also contemplated the necessity for taking up peaceful change as the next step, and did its best to combat the growing tendencies towards economic nationalism and to secure acceptance for policies of international economic co-operation. In this it was not successful, and was from the outset strongly resisted by the Conservative Party, which, even then, was anxious to join in the orgy of economic nationalism which has since afflicted the world.

Nevertheless, it is generally admitted that in the two and a quarter years during which the

[1] See Appendix IV.

[2] See Appendix V.

second Labour Government held office, it worked steadily to increase the authority and prestige of the League, and left the League stronger and world peace more secure than they had been when it came into office. Out of nine points in the foreign policy of the second Labour Government when it came into office, eight were successfully carried out, and the ninth—the Disarmament Conference—was in hand, for the date of the Conference had actually been fixed and its President designated before the Labour Government went out of office in August, 1931.

The Labour Party is determined that the third Labour Government is to be a Government in power as well as in office. The world situation is so grave that the next Labour Government will have to give a big lead if the world is to be saved from catastrophe. The Labour Party has been preparing assiduously to put itself in a position to give that lead. The policy set forth in the succeeding pages describes the nature of these preparations, for it gives in considerable detail the foreign policy to which the Labour Party is pledged. That policy, it will be seen, begins by resolutely facing up to the fact that a new arms race is well under way, and that the continuance of that race will inevitably lead to a return to the Balance of Power, which, in its turn, will infallibly end once more in war as attempts to maintain the Balance of Power have always ended throughout history and are bound to end by the very nature of the case. There is one way, and one way only, to break the vicious circle of the arms race, and that is to make a reality of the collective peace system.

That is why Labour's foreign policy is based on that system. Every party in the State professes to base its policy on the League. But Labour not only knows the heavy price that must be paid for peace but is prepared to pay that price. Labour means business with the League and peace, and adopts an attitude on these vital issues that is fundamentally different from the attitude of the older parties.

CHAPTER IV

THE FOUNDATIONS OF PEACE

STATESMANSHIP generally, in its approach to the question of international peace, has dealt with it almost exclusively as a problem of preventing war. This is to take too narrow and too shallow a view.

The League of Nations is the instrument of Labour's foreign policy: the Covenant and the Briand-Kellogg Pact are its basis. Putting an end to the arms race is its immediate objective. Progress towards disarmament is bound up with the League's success in organizing the régime of equality and mutual aid within which lies security against war.

But the peace of the world is not securely founded upon purely political measures of this character. The foundations of peace are moral, social, and economic, and Labour's peace policy consequently looks to measures more fundamental than the devising of purely political safeguards against war.

That is why there is an intimate connexion between Labour's home and foreign policy. World planning and world control of international economic life both postulate and follow from nationalized planning and socialized control of national life. The inevitable corollary to a national policy which aims at the creation of a Socialist community is an international policy which is directed towards the establishment of a Co-operative World Commonwealth. Such a policy is the only effective alternative to the arms race and the only basis for disarmament. British Labour would put this country's influence, in its dealings with all other countries, behind a truly international policy, which will develop the League of Nations in the direction of world government. The problems of a world organized as a system of sovereign States are not primarily problems of political relationships, but those arising from the conflict of private economic interests, the industrial and commercial competition between countries arising out of the desire for monopoly markets or sources of raw materials and aggravated by different social standards and different conceptions of social justice. A foreign policy which concerns itself exclusively with the political relationships of sovereign States and takes no account of the causes of economic conflict cannot be called an effective policy, nor can it build a collective peace system upon stable foundations.

In the discussion of the problem of organizing the world for peace, it is too often forgotten that the Peace Conference linked with the League of Nations the International Labour Organization, and that the constitution of the latter body explicitly declares that peace, which the League of Nations will seek to establish, must be based on social justice, and that there are in the world conditions of labour which involve ' such injustice, hardship and privation to large numbers of people as to produce unrest so great that the peace and harmony of the world are imperilled.'

British Labour agrees with this analysis. But we contend—and the post-war history of the world has emphasized and reinforced our contention—that the only way of establishing social justice is to replace the system of production for profit by a system of production for the use of the community. We hold it to be proved that the conditions resulting from the profit-making system of production not only give rise to social injustices and social inequalities that imperil peace, but also breed vested interests whose scramble for markets and for fields of investment are a direct cause of war.

As long as economic enterprise is dominated by the profit-seeking motive the peace of nations will remain in jeopardy. Under the stimulus of this motive almost every country's economic policy is assuming a nationalist and militarist character. International co-operation in the economic sphere has practically ceased : foreign trade is regulated, by means of tariffs, quotas, and licences, with the object of making the country independent, as far as this is possible, of other countries, and to strengthen its economic position at their expense. Economic nationalism, as it is called, is quite plainly a policy of national defence. The measures this policy dictates are precisely those which would be adopted by countries that expect to be involved in war. And they are measures which, like armaments, enormously increase the risks they are intended to avert. Hence the imperative need for a drastic change in the economic system if peace is to be made secure.

The international policy of Labour is in sharp contrast to these tendencies towards national isolation and economic self-sufficiency as a programme of militaristic self-defence. We challenge both the domestic and the foreign application of the doctrine of economic nationalism. In home policy it has led to highly questionable developments of the principles of national planning in regard to market control, regulation of imports, and large-scale subsidization of industries and services, with no accompanying developments in the direction of public ownership or democratic organization of the industries and services which are receiving direct and indirect financial assistance from the State. In its application to other countries it has indisputably increased the tension of international relationships and has intensified the economic antagonisms and the financial and commercial difficulties which tempt governments to seek a solution in war.

British Labour offers as an alternative the

solution embodied in its policy for both domestic and world affairs, as it is profoundly convinced that this is the only effective way, not merely of preventing war, but of laying the foundations of universal and enduring peace. That is, a peace that is more than an armed truce or a precarious and uneasy equipoise of militarized States—a world *organized* for peace on the secure foundations which the practice of international co-operation will afford. The economic and social programme which constitutes Labour's home policy is an essential instrument of our peace policy. On the one hand, the measures of economic and social reconstruction we propose lay the axe at the roots of war; on the other hand, they cannot be fully carried out nor finally consolidated except by world action. We are committed to far-reaching measures of international co-operation to render practicable and secure our economic and social policy at home, and in order to lay the social and economic foundations of peace.

What does international co-operation mean? As we conceive it, it means utilizing to the fullest extent the entire machinery and resources of the League—its economic, financial, transit and health organizations, and the International Labour Organization. Just as at home we shall endeavour to bring under control the whole economic life of the country, so in international policy we shall strive for world planning, world action, and world control in economic and financial matters, raw materials, transport, migration, travel and communications, hours of labour and conditions of employment, public health and every other matter of common international concern.

By a series of bold practical measures we must move towards the goal of a Co-operative World Commonwealth. They will strengthen the foundations of Socialism. But these are also the foundations of peace. In the degree in which we can succeed in socializing the economic activities of mankind we shall diminish the risks of war. In doing this we shall be acting upon the principles and following the indications of the Covenant of the League, and employing for its declared purpose the machinery of the League and the International Labour Organization. If we show at the same time that the triumph of Socialism is the only way to ensure world peace, we do no more than prove what the common sense of mankind already recognizes : even to wage war in the modern world, as experience has shown, nations must resort to the organization of their material resources on socialistic lines, suspending 'for the duration' the principles and practices of the capitalist economy : and much more necessary is it to invoke Socialist principles if we would organize the world for peace, or even if we would emerge from the economic depression and put a stop to the arms race.

In some fields such as public health, the suppression of social evils, transport and communications and kindred questions, the lines of great future developments are already clear. In particular, broadcasting and civil aviation will play an important part in bettering international relations by bringing the peoples of widely separated nations into closer contact and by promoting better understanding and more unity of purpose among the nations as a whole. Labour will therefore endeavour to free these great new public services from the shackles which nationalism and militarism would lay upon them.

It will likewise seek to promote every useful form of economic and financial co-operation. The frenzied and mutually contradictory measures which economic nationalism has dictated to governments that are striving to protect their peoples from the effects of the world crisis have only served to make the crisis worse. It is the declared purpose of the Labour Party to seek to bring the monetary machine under control, and thus to enable us to stabilize by international agreement both the value of money and (consequently) the rates of foreign exchange ; to supervise and control, with the aid of the Financial Committee of the League of Nations and a reformed Bank of International Settlements, the export of capital and the raising of international loans ; and to restart the flow of international trade now clogged and misdirected by tariffs and other governmental restrictions and regulations. Labour will not seek to re-establish the old *laisser-faire* system which capitalism, in its expanding phase, found convenient, but will work for the all-round lowering of tariff barriers and the substitution for these of a system of planned international exchange of goods and services which will mutually benefit workers and consumers in all countries. Such a policy would enable every country to enjoy its full share of the material abundance the world's productive system can now provide. It is in this direction that we must move to increase the volume of international trade, and by bold Socialist measures at home, in conjunction with a planned system of international trade, we can stimulate and expand consumption and help to solve the problem of unemployment all the world over, particularly in our own exporting and shipping industries and in the primary industries, especially agriculture, abroad.

As a necessary step towards a planned international economy, Labour will propose to give the economic and financial organization of the League the requisite resources and facilities to conduct a full long-term scientific inquiry into the fundamental problems of the world's economic life. This inquiry, attacked in the true spirit of scientific statesmanship, need not be unduly prolonged; some of the conclusions reached will become a matter of immediate international action; and the ultimate purpose will be to frame a coherent and fully articulated plan, for national and international application, by which the

thousands of millions of wealth now left un-
produced every year, wasted, or deliberately
destroyed when produced, will be brought to
the service of the peoples of all countries. International planning will, it may be confidently
expected, reveal possibilities of economic expan-
sion and development, to the mutual benefit of
all the nations concerned, that should help to
distract attention from sterile frontier squabbles,
and to lay the foundations for a new order of
things in Europe and the world.

In the work of economic planning, now a
plain and imperative necessity, Labour will
associate the International Labour Organization.
Its co-operation is vitally important. The rapid
development of machinery and power production,
and the attendant processes of 'rationalization'
in industry, are creating new problems affecting
the life and labour of the producing classes. At
the very time when mechanical invention, power
equipment, and scientific methods have transformed industry, and have enormously enlarged
productive capacity, the industrial and social
standards which the Trade Unions have established, and are striving to maintain, are being
challenged by capitalist employers, who allege
that the maintenance of these standards is too
costly for industry to bear. Not merely is there
a stubborn resistance to proposals for reducing
hours of work as a method of more equitably
distributing opportunities of employment, but an
attempt is being made in some countries to
destroy the working-class organization which

protects the wage-earning class ; in other countries
to weaken that organization ; in all countries to
frustrate its purpose and defeat its efforts. So
that now, more than ever, it is necessary to assist
the Trade Unions to safeguard the industrial
standards that have been established and to
strengthen these standards by developing to the
utmost the policy of regulating by international
legislation the conditions under which goods
entering into international commerce are
produced.

Labour will seek, therefore, to use the machinery
of the International Labour Organization for the
purpose it was designed to serve—namely, to
frame a code of international labour laws which
will bring industrial and social standards in all
countries up to the level of the highest. It will
also prevent them being undermined by unfair
competition in the world market from countries
which seek to gain advantage by debasing standards of wages and conditions of employment
for their own people. In our view the International Labour Organization has not yet been
used to the full extent that it should be and can
be, to assist in bringing about a more humane,
enlightened and socially just, economic and
industrial system.

In this way, and in no other way, is it possible,
in Labour's view, to lay the common economic
and social foundations for a Peace-World, in
which alone civilization can survive. But these
are also the foundations of Socialism. We are
Socialists because we can see no other way of

organizing the world for peace, because a comprehensive policy of socialization at home and of active international co-operation for the development of common interests overriding every nationalist and imperialist interest can alone remove the causes of war.

CHAPTER V

DISARMAMENT AND NATIONAL DEFENCE

THE race in armaments is once more in full swing. It is the most dangerous symptom of the steady deterioration of the international situation that has set in since September, 1931.

Every one knows that the race in armaments is a vicious circle, and every one knows that its ultimate end is—war.

But those who advocate bigger armaments do so in the name of their necessity for national defence. Their argument in this and other countries is invariably the same : ' We have disarmed to a dangerous degree ; the others have failed to follow our example ; they have begun rearming ; therefore, we have no alternative but to follow suit. In any case the whole world knows that we do not want war, nor do we dream of attacking any one. Our armaments are purely for defence and cannot possibly be interpreted by other nations as a threat ; whereas we are doubtful about the purpose for which other countries are arming and cannot risk giving them the benefit of the doubt.' It is necessary to face the hard fact that these arguments are actually being used and are sincerely believed in by the

D

peoples concerned, in every State taking part in the new arms race, just as they were used with equal sincerity on both sides of the arms race that culminated in August, 1914.

The new arms race is already overshadowing, and if suffered to continue will break down, the collective peace system and revive the conditions of international anarchy and the Balance of Power, with the results that have invariably been produced by these conditions. The alternative to the arms race and Armageddon is to make a reality of the collective peace system to which we are bound by solemn treaty obligations, and for which the world paid the price of four years of the most terrible war in human history.

An integral part of the peace-keeping system is the obligation to reduce and limit arms. Fifteen years' struggle by the League with this problem, including three heart-breaking years of the Disarmament Conference, have made it plain beyond any possibility of doubt that the arms race can be stopped and the towering armaments that threaten civilization can be abolished only if there be (a) a complete system for settling disputes by pacific means ; (b) stringent obligations to take joint action against an aggressor so thoroughly worked out as to be as nearly fool- and knave-proof as is possible in any human institution, and inspiring general confidence that they will, when it comes to the point, be applied. If a nation believes itself exposed to the danger of being overwhelmed in war by a more powerful enemy, it will not refrain from making the most complete preparations, which its resources permit, against the danger of attack. The principal political condition for disarmament is that States should not have to rely on their unaided strength for defence, but should be able to rely on the organized collective action of the League so long as they behave as loyal members of the League.

To work out, and pledge ourselves to such collective obligations is not an easy or light task. But we must choose to-day between two alternatives, either of which is disagreeable and risky: we can either go back to the old idea first proclaimed by a Roman general and a favourite maxim ever since of men of war: ' If you want peace, prepare for war.' That method in the last analysis rests on contradictory arguments, on an attempt to perform the impossible feat of each State being stronger than its neighbour. It entails the reversion to international anarchy, the Balance of Power and the arms race. It can hardly be called a risk because it has throughout history proved a certainty. It always has ended in war and always will. Its advocates indeed proclaim that war is inevitable, and if their paradoxical method of pursuing peace be adopted they will undoubtedly prove themselves true prophets.

The alternative is to go all out in making a reality of the collective defence system. That is a colossal task. It requires daring, imagination, a steadfast purpose—every bit of the brains and pluck and political genius of the British people. But as John Stuart Mill once put it: ' Against great ills small remedies do not produce small effects—they produce no effect at all.' The arms race is a great ill. It is an ill so terrible and big with such black disaster that we can make no impression on it by half measures. It is no good standing with one foot in the Balance of Power and the other in the League of Nations, paying lip service to the League, but refusing to accept any more peace commitments. The only result of such ambiguous toying with the destinies of civilization is the steady piling up of more war commitments in the shape of bigger and bigger armaments and an accelerating arms race. That kind of policy makes the worst of both worlds. There is something to be said, although it happens to be wrong, for leaving the League and reverting to isolation. There is a great deal to be said and, Labour believes, rightly said, for going all out to make a success of the League. But there is nothing to be said for remaining in the League in such a faint-hearted and lukewarm manner that we let it fail and are dragged down in its failure. Those who find insuperable difficulties in any vigorous policy shut their eyes to the awful risk, nay, the certainty of ultimate disaster involved in having no policy, or what amounts to no policy. Events are moving with portentous swiftness and he who attempts to stand still is really going backwards. The drift towards war has already acquired such momentum that the only way to stop it is by a tremendous drive for peace. To smash the vicious circle of the arms race requires heroic remedies.

These are the central truths on which Labour bases its policy for disarmament and defence. That is why Labour would take immediate steps to put an end to the race in armaments and the growing danger of war. Labour would submit to all nations at Geneva a bold and far-reaching plan both for all-round disarmament and for the international organization of security.

The plan will provide for :

(a) the abolition of all the arms (warships over 10,000 tons, submarines and aircraft carriers, military and naval aviation, tanks and guns over 4-inch calibre, with strict limitation of smaller arms) forbidden to the Central Powers by the 1919 Treaties, with a system of regular supervision and diplomatic, economic and financial guarantees of execution ;

(b) the limitation of armaments' budgets ;

(c) the abolition of national air forces, the internationalizing of civil aviation, and the creation of an international air police force;

(d) the nationalization and drastic international control of the manufacture of and trade in arms ;

(e) a treaty of non-aggression, clarified by a definition of aggression and linked with the sanctions system of the League ; the revision of the Covenant to incorporate in it the complete renunciation of war contained in the Briand-Kellogg Pact ; the bringing into force of the Treaty of Financial Assistance

and the Treaty for Strengthening the Means
to Prevent War ;
(f) machinery and obligations for settling all
disputes by pacific means.

The ultimate object of Labour's disarmament
and security policy is to abolish all national armed
forces and to entrust the defence of world law
and order to an international police force, under
the League of Nations.

There is abundant evidence that a programme
on these lines has the support of a large majority
of British opinion.   The experience of the Disarmament Conference further shows that it would
have the support of a big majority of the nations
represented there.   It is impossible, of course, to
predict precisely what the international situation
will be when the next Labour Government assumes
office, but the main lines of development are likely
to remain unaffected, and a plan like that sketched
will still have a great deal of support, for the
simple reason that it is the only way out of the
tragic dilemma of the arms race.

Labour's policy on disarmament and defence,
it must be remembered, is only part of a wider
policy which will be applied simultaneously all
along the line.   At the same time as we shall
be pressing on with disarmament and collective
defence, we shall be laying the economic foundations of peace and facing such issues as the
problem of peaceful change in Europe ; the
menace to peace in the Far East ; the revival of
militant nationalism and the cult of war in the

world. Labour's way of treating these issues is discussed in subsequent chapters.

To sum up : the question of national defence is once more a burning problem for our country and for all other countries. Some voices are raised in favour of unilateral disarmament and non-resistance—i.e., of abandoning self-defence altogether. But such views are not likely to be held by a sufficient number of people to bring them within the horizon of practical politics. Apart from the repugnance felt by most people to the whole conception of surrender and abdication, an attitude of this sort would not solve the problem of peace in a world where there are such great and tragic examples of the use and the glorification of force and fraud, and where nations are so interdependent that pacifists who reject economic ' sanctions '[1] thereby become, willy-nilly, accessories after the fact to the crime of war, for they are in favour of selling war materials to an aggressor. For good or ill, therefore, we must face the problem of national defence. There are only two ways of solving that problem. One is to revert to the traditional conception of each nation being sole judge of its rights and, therefore, solely responsible for their defence. In pursuance of that conception our frontiers would run wherever the multitudinous rights of the world-wide British Empire were liable to serious challenge from States who in their turn would

---

[1] Sanctions are the measures provided in Article 16 of the Covenant for cutting off relations with a peace-breaker.

be arming in response to our armaments. Those would be impossibly large and ill-defined commitments, and moreover they would grow more numerous and more onerous in an atmosphere of deepening suspicion and fear till the strain of the arms race was broken by another great war. On these lines, the more we and other nations spend on defence, the more insecure we shall all become, and the more we should between us be preparing the world not for peace but for war.

The other way is to make a reality of the method of pooled defence by putting the whole power of the British Empire behind the League in exchange for other countries doing the same. This new method means that we have only one frontier—the Covenant, which guarantees us, on the basis of reciprocity, that if our territory be invaded, or if third party judgement on our rights be flouted, we shall have the world on our side against the aggressor. That is a limited and manageable commitment. On this basis it will become possible drastically to reduce, limit, control and ultimately internationalize armaments. On these lines the more the nations organize their collective national defence, the safer we shall all become and the more remote will be the danger of war.

The new method involves the risk of trusting at least some other nations (so does an alliance) and of third party judgement on our rights. But it affords a reasonable chance of getting rid of war altogether. It is the method to which we are pledged by treaty obligations that it cost ten million dead and twenty million wounded to bring into existence.   We owe it to the dead, as well as to the living, to put our frontier in the Covenant and our national defence behind our frontier.

In his maiden speech to the Assembly (on September 18, 1934) M. Litvinov, chief delegate of the Soviet Union, said :

'The sound and the meaning of the words "organization of peace" ought now to be different from their sound and meaning twelve or fifteen years ago.   Then, to many members of the League of Nations, war seemed to be a remote theoretical danger, and there seemed to be no hurry as to its prevention.   Now, war must appear to all as the threatening danger of to-morrow.   Now the organization of peace, for which so far very little has been done, must be set against the extremely active organization of war.   Then, many believed that the spirit of war might be exorcised by adjurations, resolutions and declarations.   Now, everybody knows that the exponents of the idea of war, the open promulgators of the refashioning of the map of Europe and Asia by the sword, are not to be intimidated by paper obstacles.   Members of the League of Nations know this by experience. We are now confronted with the task of averting war by more effective means.'

Admiral Sir Herbert Richmond, in a book published in October, 1934,[1] points out with regard to the machinery of peace :

[1] *Sea Power in the Modern World*.

' The " Pax Britannica " or of any other kind results from the fixed determination that peace *shall* be preserved, not from a platonic affection and desire for peace.   It is the result of a will, not a pious wish.'

Labour agrees with both these statements : peace cannot be preserved by words alone, but only by the collective organization of effective means.   Those means will be provided by putting national armaments at the service of peace.   What is wanted, in order to achieve this, is a real will to peace, a fixed determination that peace *shall* be preserved, coupled with a clear realization of the fact that the only true safety is the safety of all, because unless national provisions for defence are directed to and work towards this specific end, they will become a source of antagonism and, therefore, of increasing peril.

The world-wide British Commonwealth is scattered over the seven seas and the five continents in an interdependent world where war anywhere may become war everywhere; the " Pax Britannica " is inextricably bound up with the peace of the world.

CHAPTER VI

CHANGING THE STATUS QUO

FROM the outset of the enterprise of organizing peace, voices have been raised in warning against the danger of stereotyping the *status quo*. It is pointed out that war, terrible as it is, is a way of changing acquired rights. There is no means of international legislation, and so the forces of change—growth in populations, economic developments leading to conflicts over access to markets or raw materials, etc.—bank up until they accumulate enough explosive force to break out in war.

So the argument runs. It is generally followed up by objections to any system of sanctions (collective defence) unless it is accompanied by some procedure for effecting changes in treaty rights. At this point the argument gets a little confused, for it identifies sanctions with ' stereotyping the *status quo*,' although sanctions come into operation only against a State that has *resorted to war*. In other words, those who object to sanctions on the ground that they ' stereotype the *status quo* ' are really demanding that war be retained as an instrument of national policy, though so little are most of them aware of this fact that they ask that the Kellogg-Briand

Pact (which renounces resort to war as an instrument of national policy) instead of the Covenant
should be the basis for organizing peace !

Some members of this school, however, frankly
face the fact that they are asking that war be
retained as the final arbiter. They justify this
attitude by arguing that fear induced by threats
of war may be the best way of compelling States
to revise their frontiers or other treaty rights, and
that the present peace settlement is so bad that
they are not prepared to maintain it against
change, even if that change be effected by war.
And so they protest, not only against sanctions,
but against closing the ' gap ' in the Covenant
and against all-in arbitration.

Few of those who advance this view explain
precisely what are the changes in the existing
status quo which they hope will be brought about
by retaining the power to threaten war. As a
rule they simply assume that the injustices of the
Peace Treaties are so glaring and so undisputed
that no one of goodwill can have any trouble in
saying what these injustices are and how they
should be put right. In particular they assume
that the re-drawing of the map of Europe will
cause no trouble to any one whose genuine purpose is the establishment of lasting peace.

Many good people of liberal views, including
many of the Liberal Party, which in 1924 held the
balance of power in the House of Commons,
condemned the Geneva Protocol by the very
argument here under discussion, that it would
' stereotype the *status quo.*' In so doing they

were instinctively reacting against what they held
to be the plain indisputable wrongs which the
Treaties of Peace had perpetrated against the
defeated nations.

But were their assumptions justified ? Could
they have re-drawn the map as easily as they
believed ? Could they have found new frontiers
which would have been approved by the universal
conscience as self-evidently just ? Nothing could
be more improbable. The truth is that the
populations of Europe are not divided into
homogeneous groups of identical racial origin
and complete community of interest. On the
contrary, Central and Southern Europe is a
mosaic of mixed populations, differing in race,
religion and language. If the principle of race,
or President Wilson's principle of self-determina-
tion be adopted, there are in many places *no*
frontiers that are right, *no* mere changing of
existing territorial arrangements that will remove
existing injustices without creating new injustices
that may be worse. Sovereignty rather than
frontiers is what requires revising.

Still less can those who advance the argument
now under consideration justify their second
assumption that the changes required in the
status quo can be brought about by war or threat
of war. For this assumption challenges the whole
of history. The verdict of war goes to the
strong, not necessarily to him whose cause is just.
War throughout the ages has brought the injustice
from which new wars are bred. If good results
have also sometimes followed, it has always been

plain that they could have been obtained far
better, far more cheaply and far more enduringly
without war than with it.

Certainly at the present time the Socialist will
not accept this argument about stereotyping the
status quo.　He will hold fast to the fundamental
reality of the modern world, which is that civilization must stamp out war or war will destroy
civilization ; war cannot be retained as an instrument of change, for war cannot be localized or
its destructive effects limited, nor can peace be
organized on the basis of the right to go to war.
Therefore, whatever the merits of any dispute,
war must be forbidden and ruled out absolutely
as a method of settlement.

Nor will the Socialist accept the argument of
another school who desire to organize sanctions,
but who wish at the same time to set up some sort
of ' Court of Equity ' with compulsory jurisdiction.　By this is apparently meant that a body of
men should be appointed with the power to decree
such changes in the territorial and other established rights of States as seemed good to them.
The decisions of these men would be able to
override international law and treaty obligations.
Sanctions and ' compulsory equity ' would be
imposed on a world of sovereign States.

To this school the Socialist will reply that the
method they propose for securing change in the
existing *status quo* is wholly impracticable.　For
they propose to leave untouched the ' sovereignty '
and ' independence ' of each State over the territory subjected to its rule ; yet they also propose

that sovereign States should surrender their territory at the bidding of a ' Court of Equity,' untrammelled by law and free to override all existing rights which governments by treaty or custom have acquired. What hope is there that the governments of sovereign States will, in fact, agree to anything of the kind? It has been possible to induce them to submit the interpretation of their rights to the test of third party judgement operating on the basis of law. But this proposal for a ' Court of Equity ' goes far beyond that. It would mean that governments must accept ' legislation,' the changing of existing legal rights, by a body in which they have no representation. Such ' legislation without representation ' would strike at the vital principle of sovereignty and, therefore, it may be confidently predicted that the governments of sovereign States, in the world as it is to-day, will not accept it.

Nor will the Socialist much regret that this is so. For to him it appears that both these schools of thought fall into confusion and contradiction because they do not go to the root of the problem of securing justice and peaceful change. They are trying to devise means of organizing peace without touching on the sovereignty or the economic and social foundations of States. That is an enterprise akin to squaring the circle. It is not so much frontiers that matter as the political and economic régimes within the frontiers, and the way in which these régimes link on with each other across frontiers.

The whole Socialist approach to this question

of peaceful change of the *status quo* is, indeed, quite different. To begin with, we hold that the primary cause of war in the modern world is economic. There is weighty support for this view in the analysis of world conditions made in the first section of this book. But a direct opinion on this subject is worth quoting, for it emanates from the eminent Belgian Prime Minister, who is also an industrialist and financier, M. Theunis, who presided over the World Economic Conference of 1927 at Geneva. In his presidential address M. Theunis said : ' Economic conflicts and divergence of economic interests are perhaps the most serious and the most permanent of all the dangers which are likely to threaten the peace of the world. No machinery for the settlement of international disputes can be relied upon to maintain peace if the economic policies of the world so develop as to create not only deep divergencies of economic interest between different masses of the world's population, but a sense of intolerable injury and injustice. No task is more urgent or more vital than that of securing agreement on certain principles of policy which are necessary in the interests of future peace. And there is perhaps no question which, in comparison with its intrinsic importance, has had so little careful and collective deliberation.'

Sir Arthur Salter, who quotes this opinion with approval,[1] adds : ' In a word, if we want peace

[1] In a lecture printed in ' Problems of Peace,' Third Series, being the proceedings of the Geneva Institute of International Relations, 1928.

we must not merely rely upon a machinery for the settlement of disputes when they arise ; we must so lay the foundations of peace that the disputes which do arise will be relatively un-envenomed by previous dissension, and will not be deeply rooted in a long-standing sense of divergent interest and injustice. . . . If we, comfortably believing that there is a machinery for stopping war, are content to allow the economic forces of the world to move along lines which lead and guide to war, even the machinery of the League will not, at the last moment, save us from the consequences.'

Those words were spoken in 1928. Since then the economic depression has released tremendous economic and social forces, the character and political repercussions of which were indicated in the first two chapters of this book. How Labour proposes to grapple with these forces is described in Chapter IV—' The Foundations of Peace.' In laying the foundations of peace, it must be observed, Labour is at the same time laying the foundations of a new type of society, a world-wide and dynamic society that will be changing and growing rapidly, for it will be based on the active and fruitful principles of co-operation and social justice.

But the social and economic forces released by the great depression have led to a revival of militant nationalism and aggressive policies, and these in turn have started a new race in armaments. So far from there being any reason for anxiety about the *status quo*—either political, social,

E

economic, financial, or international—being stereotyped, there is grave reason to fear that the forces of change may become so violent as to shatter civilization. The world is moving with a blind and distracted motion, but moving rapidly ; it does not know where it is going, but it is certainly not standing still. So far from treaties proving too rigid, they are losing all sanctity. It seems misplaced, or at least mistimed, anxiety to worry about stereotyping the *status quo* when the world is in the melting pot, and all things are in flux.

That is why Labour wishes to bend its energies first to stop civilization being swept away in the cataclysm of war. Unless this can be done, there is little hope of securing the kind of changes by which present injustices can be removed. Merely to speak of ' Treaty Revision,' as some people do, as if the treaties could be scrapped and replaced overnight by others embodying territorial frontiers more to the liking of the defeated powers, is to play with words, and with dangerous words at that. For such ' Treaty Revision,' if it were attempted in the present con-ditions and in the present atmosphere in Europe, would end in war. Such ' Revision ' is not, as many people too confidingly believe, a way to get rid of the running sores in the international body politic ; on the contrary, it is the surest way to provoke a conflict which, by wise handling, may yet be avoided.

But if this direct onslaught on the Revision problem be ruled out, how can we hope to secure the peaceful changes in the existing *status quo* which assuredly will be required if present grievances are ever to be removed ?

The first thing to do is to stop the arms race. That can be done only by the adoption of a plan for collective defence, disarmament, and the creation of an international police force, such as that outlined in the previous chapter.

The adoption of a plan on these lines would transform the political atmosphere in Europe, by restoring faith in the rule of law and banishing the fear that violence would be used to effect changes in national territories. In that atmosphere much can be done by agreement and negotiation and by utilizing the means of moral pressure and discussion provided by the machinery of the League of Nations.

There are three possible ways in which change might be effected through the machinery of the League.

The first is by the use of Article 19 of the Covenant, which is designed to promote ' the reconsideration by Members of the League of treaties which have become inapplicable and the consideration of international conditions whose continuance might " endanger the peace of the world." '

Many people believe that this Article has been tried and failed, and that it is as good as dead. Nothing could be further from the truth. The Article has never been invoked by any European power. On the other hand, the Assembly has discussed the Article and its meaning on a number of occasions. In general the tendency has been towards a restrictive interpretation of its provisions. But none of the powers which it provides has been in any way compromised, and if it were properly used it might prove to be an instrument of considerable power. Under its terms any member of the League can bring up any existing international arrangement in which it would desire a change, and could insist upon a full public discussion. The Assembly, by majority vote, could appoint a Commission of Inquiry to investigate the issues involved ; this commission, when appointed, could make a report and recommendations by a majority of its members ; when it received this report the Assembly (again by majority vote, since this is only a question of ' advice ' and not decision) could make any proposals to the parties which it might find wise. It can hardly be doubted that this procedure would bring the pressure of world public opinion to bear very effectively against the maintenance of arrangements condemned by the conscience of mankind.

The second method of obtaining peaceful change might be through the use of Article 15 of the Covenant. In connexion with the proposals to amend the Covenant so as to rule out resort to war altogether, the idea received a great deal of support that members of the League should agree to accept a report of the Council under Article 15, paragraph 6, or of the Assembly under Article 15, paragraph 10. These reports dispense with the votes of the parties (and, in the case of

the Assembly, only the votes of the States represented on the Council and of a bare majority of
the other members of the Assembly are required),
and as they may recommend changes in the legal
rights of the parties, an amendment on these lines
would constitute the beginnings of international
legislation.

The third method by which peaceful change
might be obtained is through reference to the
Permanent Court of International Justice at The
Hague. The Permanent Court, like any other
court, is competent to hear cases arising from the
claim that circumstances have so changed as to
make release from treaty or other legal obligations
necessary (this competence derives from the well-
known principle of international law : *rebus sic
stantibus*[1]). The Court itself, if freely used under
the Optional Clause, may build up a series of
judgements and opinions which would constitute
a form of judicial legislation by putting new con-
structions on treaties and on principles of international law. It may be added that an increasing
number of League treaties provide for their own
reconsideration and if necessary revision at stated
periods and on specified conditions, and the
League is constantly holding conferences which
conclude new treaties.

Thus, it is fair to claim that the forces of
growth and change, if the channel of war is
successfully blocked, may be trusted to find for

[1] This principle was unsuccessfully invoked before
the Court by France in her case with Switzerland over
the free zones round Geneva.

themselves new channels and avenues of development. The League, as an association of States, is subject to the same tendencies as any other confederation or federal system, namely, the tendency to provide for means of legislation even at the cost of surrender of sovereign powers by the units in the association in order to make the system work and to meet the clamant needs of everyday life.

But it may be predicted that in proportion as the community of nations begins to devise methods approaching international legislation to promote its common interests, it will be found that such legislation will be concerned not so much with shifting frontiers as with the real interests of the community, that is, the lives and fortunes of the men and women on both sides of whatever frontier may run through the area affected by the proposed legislation.

It may further be predicted that legislation in the international as in the national domain will be based on the representation of the community concerned and not camouflaged as a 'Court of Equity' imposing its decisions from outside.

The analogy at the back of the Socialist's mind when he considers the problem of peaceful change is always the analogy with confederations and federal systems. Labour is thinking in terms of the dawn of world government.

That is why it would be, in the Labour view, a mistake to suppose that peaceful change can ever consist principally in frontier revisions between sovereign States. It is sovereignty itself that must change. The greatest peaceful change must be the progressive disappearance of inflamed nationalism and the growth of international arrangements across frontiers on tariffs, currency, economic co-operation, transport, and, in the political field, on the fair treatment of minorities.

There was much in the history of the first ten years of the League to encourage us to believe that such change can be hoped for, and to show us how fast and far it may go once the fear of war has been eliminated from international life. Once that fear is gone, and those kinds of changes have begun, some frontier revision may also become possible and wise.

The policy of Labour will favour any just and reasonable frontier adjustments and treaty revisions. But Labour's main effort in the domain of changing the *status quo* will be concentrated on banishing the fear of war, laying the economic foundations of peace, social justice, and co-operation, and abolishing frontiers by drawing the nations together into a World Commonwealth. In so far as the world is not yet ready for such a transformation, we shall begin with whatever States will share our ideal and join with us in advancing step by step towards the common goal.

CHAPTER VII

THE FAR EAST

LABOUR follows with deepening anxiety the course of events in the Far East, and has never failed to appreciate the extreme gravity of the situation. It regards the problem of Asia as pivotal to the peace of the world. It recognizes that there exists to-day a condition of stalemate which is full of danger. The aggression on the part of Japan, and the general disregard of solemn treaty obligations have had dire consequences in international relations. In this connexion it is interesting to note that *The Times*, in its leading article of October 4, 1934, observes :

'There cannot . . . be any real doubt that the primary causes of the upward tendency of armaments have been Japanese policy in the Far East and the deliberate rearmament of Germany under the Hitler régime.'

Though events in Germany have partly reflected the inability of the Geneva conference to give effect to the principle of equality of rights in a system of security, there is a strong feeling in Labour circles that the primary cause of the failure of the Disarmament Conference to reach success has been the loss of confidence in collective security occasioned by the Far Eastern situation.

Labour has officially declared that its first objective would be to do everything within its power to remove the menace of a great war in that part of the world. It would take its stand squarely on the Covenant of the League of Nations, the Nine-Power Treaty[1] and the Pact of Paris, as interpreted in the unanimous report of the League Assembly concerning the Manchurian dispute. It would keep in closest touch with the United States and the Soviet Union with regard to a concerted attitude against aggression and the violation of treaties in the Far East. It would make clear that any fresh resort to war would be met by world-wide action on the basis of the treaties forbidding war. Moreover, Labour would use all its influence to frustrate any effort to make China the victim of imperialist exploitation or to extort acquiescence in the violation of China's territorial integrity and political independence. It would also endeavour to secure by common action those conditions under which alone a reasonable standard of life is attainable by the peoples of the East.

The Assembly Report by which Great Britain is bound makes it clear that (1) Manchuria is an integral part of China, under Chinese sovereignty, and the Nine-Power Treaty applies to Manchuria as it does to every other part of China. (2) The present military occupation of Manchuria is the result of Japanese military operations that cannot

[1] See Appendix VI.

be called defensive and for which China has no responsibility; the existence of this occupation is a standing violation of Article 10[1] of the Covenant and Article 1 of the Nine-Power Treaty. (3) The present régime in Manchuria was created and is controlled by the Japanese General Staff; its maintenance and recognition are contrary to the interests of China and to the wishes of the population, which is ninety-five per cent Chinese; its existence is a violation of the Covenant, Nine-Power Treaty and Paris Pact, and incompatible with the maintenance of peace in the Far East. (4) The maintenance of peace in the Far East is a matter of international concern.

The report recommended that Manchuria be demilitarized and restored to Chinese rule on a semi-autonomous basis and with extensive safe-guards for all legitimate Japanese rights and interests; due account was also to be taken of the position of the U.S.S.R. in North Manchuria and of the principle of the ' open door.' There should be international co-operation through the League in assisting the Chinese Government's national reconstruction plan.

Finally the report bound all the members of the League not to recognize ' Manchukuo ' *de jure* or *de facto*, to abstain from any act that might facilitate the maintenance of this treaty-breaking régime, and to concert their policy on the basis of the report. An Assembly Advisory Committee was set up, on which the United States, which accepted the report, is represented, and of which

[1] See Appendix VII.

the U.S.S.R. and Great Britain are *ex officio* members, in virtue of their membership of the Council.

The report was accepted by China and rejected by Japan. The whole issue remains open, nothing is settled, and the League's responsibility for the preservation of peace and securing respect for treaty obligations continues.

Labour's policy is to take this situation as it finds it, to apply the non-recognition policy loyally, to make effective the plan of technical co-operation with China for purposes of national reconstruction, and to keep the peace. Labour believes that if only peace can be kept, the intolerable burden of military expenditure in Japan, the ceaseless guerrilla warfare in Manchuria, the drain of making good the constant deficits in the trade balance and finances of 'Manchukuo,' the growing strength of China and the U.S.S.R., and the deepening hostility of the whole world, will in the end induce the Japanese people to recognize that the solution recommended in the Assembly Report is fair and honourable to Japan as well as to China, and is the only possible alternative to disaster for their own country.

But Labour recognizes that the present situation is neither just nor stable, and that peace is not likely to be kept unless it is known beforehand by all concerned that any fresh resort to war would certainly be visited by sanctions, applied by the whole League in association with the United States. Hence the statement that the Labour Government ' would keep in closest touch

with the United States and the Soviet Union with
regard to a concerted attitude against aggression
and the violation of treaties in the Far East. It
would make clear that any fresh resort to war
would be met by world-wide action on the basis
of the treaties forbidding war.'

This policy, it will be seen, is merely the loyal
and effective application of our treaty obligations,
as interpreted in the report by which our country,
as well as the other members of the League and
the United States, is bound, as a result of the
decision of the governments concerned.

The Lytton Report, on which the Assembly
Report is based, was everywhere hailed as a
remarkable document. It was the result of the
labours, not of theorists, but of five seasoned and
hard-headed ex-colonial governors, soldiers with
colonial experience, and diplomats, all nationals
of the great powers with interests in China; this
Commission had a large staff of experts, travelled
extensively, and had every conceivable source of
information thrown open to it and every variety
of argument pressed upon it; it visited Japan
first, and throughout its investigation it had a
Japanese assessor, as well as a plethora of Japanese
documents and elaborate Japanese surveillance
during the whole of its visit in Manchuria; the
report was unanimous. The Assembly Report
was elaborated over a period of months after the
publication of the Lytton Report, by the delegates
of nineteen Governments, including our own,
with the assistance of the Far Eastern experts
of their foreign offices, and with a full sense

of the political responsibilities involved; it accepted the findings of the Lytton Commission completely. The Assembly Report therefore represents an accumulated weight of knowledge and authority not lightly to be disregarded. The British Government accepted that report and it is still binding on this country.

Nevertheless, it would be idle to ignore that there is an undercurrent of opinion in the Conservative Party and Press and in certain quarters in the City, which wishes to disregard the Assembly Report and our treaty obligations, and to come to an understanding with Japan on the basis of condoning the occupation of Manchuria. There is hardly a debate on foreign affairs in the House in which some Conservative M.P.s and papers do not raise their voices in favour of a renewal in some form of the Anglo-Japanese alliance. In certain parts of the Conservative Press this view is advocated with remarkable persistence. There was a spate of articles, editorials and special supplements in this sense at the time of the dispatch of the F.B.I. economic mission to 'Manchukuo' almost immediately after Parliament rose in the summer of 1934. From the point of view of politicians who think in pre-war terms there is much to be said for a 'deal' with Japan: 'We are now,' their argument runs, 'in much the same position towards Japan as Great Britain was towards France before the "deal" over Morocco and Egypt, or towards Russia before the "deal" over the partitioning of Persia. To-day the alternative is an arms race leading to a war, or a deal with Japan at the expense of China coupled with a political, commercial and naval understanding.'

The trouble with this policy is that it ignores the Covenant and the Nine-Power Treaty ; it overlooks the fact that nationalism is now so strong in China that that country can no longer be submitted to the indignity of ' spheres of influence,' let alone protectorates and partition ; finally it would commit us to hostility to the Soviet Union and the United States, and be interpreted in certain powerful circles in Japan as opening the door to further military adventures.

Such a policy would make for war and not for peace. So repugnant is it, indeed, to morals and common sense that no British Government could embark on such a course. But the advocates of this policy may exert sufficient influence to prevent the vigorous pursuit of any alternative policy. That is why it is necessary to insist that here, too, it is disastrous, while remaining nominally bound by the Covenant, to adopt an attitude that encourages potential aggressors to speculate on our defaulting on our obligations when it comes to the point. That policy also makes for war and not peace. It makes the worst of both the pre-war and the post-war worlds. Under the guise of avoiding immediate risk it incurs the certainty of ultimate disaster.

The only policy capable of keeping the peace is openly to stand by our treaty obligations in deed as well as word. That is the only policy in consonance with the moral, juridical and material facts of the post-war world. It involves making it clear that ' any fresh resort to war would be met by world-wide action on the basis of the treaties forbidding war.'

To understand exactly what that means it should be realized that any war fought to maintain, let alone to extend, the present Covenant-breaking military occupation of China's north-eastern provinces (Manchuria and Jehol) must necessarily be regarded as aggressive by all States that have accepted the Assembly Report of February 24, 1933. To regard such a war as defensive would be to repudiate the Nine-Power Treaty, the Covenant, and the Paris Pact, as interpreted in the Assembly Report by which this country, the U.S.A., and all the members of the League are bound.

If Great Britain took her stand, not in any violent or challenging fashion, but firmly and unequivocally, on that position, there is no reasonable doubt that the U.S.S.R., France and Italy would follow suit, and that the U.S.A. would give its cordial approval and diplomatic support. And there is equally no reasonable doubt that the whole League would fall into line, and that as a result of this calm but clear-cut and steadfast policy peace and order would gradually be restored to the Far East.

The Assembly Report declares that it is in the interests of world peace that the League should ' continue to afford China the technical assistance in modernizing her institutions which her Government might request with a view to enabling the

Chinese people to reorganize and consolidate the Chinese State.'   In lending this assistance through the machinery of the League, the Labour Government will endeavour to promote the political and economic stability of the Chinese Republic, not in the interests of financial groups, but in the interests of the Chinese people and of the world at large. The Labour Party will reverse the imperialist policy of domination and economic exploitation which in the past has been so grave a menace to the peaceful development of the world.

In this policy the hearty co-operation of the Soviet Union and the United States may be counted upon, for the policy is at all points in conformity with the interests of these two countries and with the record and spirit of their relations with China.

It should not be forgotten that when the Great War supervened the Allied Powers appealed to China to side with them in the struggle. She responded to the call, and received in return a promise that on the termination of the war she would be accorded in international relations the position and the consideration due to a great country. The promise was given unhesitatingly, whether or no its full import was appreciated by those Powers who subscribed to it at the time. So far as China was concerned, the intention was clear. She joined the Allied cause, consistently with her policy as a whole, with the purpose of furthering her national aspirations at the first convenient moment.

A few years later, in 1922, the States signing the

Nine-Power Treaty agreed to ' provide the fullest and most unembarrassed opportunity to China to develop and maintain for herself an effective and stable Government.'

On May 22, 1926, Sir Austen Chamberlain, in a memorandum to China, laid down the principle that all the Powers ' should abandon the idea that the economic and political development of China can only be secured under foreign tutelage ' and that it should be the policy of the Powers ' to endeavour to maintain harmonious relations with China without waiting for or insisting on the prior establishment of a strong Central Government.'

In May, 1931, the Labour Government gave its cordial approval to the inauguration, at the request of the Chinese Government, of the League plan of technical co-operation with the National Economic Council, the body set up by the Chinese Government to plan and execute its programme of reconstruction. The Labour Government also took up the question of the rendition of British concessions and the abolition of exterritoriality, as had been promised at the Washington Conference and since.

In 1933, the Assembly endorsed the report of the Lytton Commission, which described how political and economic reconstruction was progressing, and how the tide of national sentiment was rising.

In 1934 the League technical agent in China, Dr. Rajchman, in a remarkable report surveyed the whole field of reconstruction and the multitudinous activities of the Government and its National Economic Council. The report brought out the

F

fact that the entire political, financial and administrative responsibility for all this work necessarily rests on the Chinese Government, that any outside help is technical and advisory in character and subsidiary in extent, and that the time when China could be in any relationship of tutelage or patronage to any foreign power or group of foreign powers or interests, has irrevocably passed. The West must adjust itself finally to the conception of equality and co-partnership in its relations with China.

400,000,000 people and 4,000 years of tradition, in a country as big as all Europe, are not easy to modernize and consolidate into a strong State. But much has been done, still more is being prepared, and the spread of the sentiment of national unity is ultimately as inevitable in China as elsewhere. The Chinese, and they alone, can build up their vast country, although their task will be facilitated by the machinery for technical co-operation ready to their hand in the League. It is the intention of British Labour to give every assistance in the power of a fellow-member of the League, because we are convinced that to do so is in the interests of the whole of mankind. We look forward eagerly to the day when the great Chinese people shall take its rightful place among the leading nations of the world.

Labour's policy for restoring law and order in the Far East is simple, and rests on feelings of equal friendship and respect for the peoples of both China and Japan. It consists of a fixed determination that peace *shall* be kept and the Covenant applied without fear or favour; a rigorous application of the policy of non-recognition of 'Manchukuo' coupled with a standing offer for a solution of the Manchurian problem honourable and fair to both parties; effective help to China in her plan of co-operation with the League. That is a policy based solidly on the facts of the situation; on our treaty obligations and on the unanimous findings of the Assembly and Lytton Commission; on enlightened self-interest, and on the claims of justice and the necessities of peace. Labour intends to give a lead on these lines, in the confident expectation of rallying such support as to make its policy prevail and to remove the present danger of war.

CHAPTER VIII

UNIVERSALITY OR REGIONAL AGREEMENTS

THE Labour Party will always strive to secure world-wide acceptance for its policy of organizing peace. On the economic side it is clear that trade and finance are world-wide, and that no policy can be more than a half-way house, if it does not cover most countries. On the side of disarmament not much can be done if even one or two powerful nations stand out, and the collective defence system will give better security at the price of smaller risks and commitments the more closely it approximates to universality. The basic principle of the League is universality, and the League can only really come into its own if it becomes truly world-wide.

But the framers of the Covenant were realists. They could not foresee the social and economic crisis, nor the recrudescence of militant nationalism and the cult of war which issued from the crisis and converted it into a world peace crisis. Nor could they know that in the second decade of the League's existence two great powers which were permanent members of its Council would leave it and that a third great power, which was one of the principal authors of the Covenant, would not yet be a member of the League.

But they took care to frame the Covenant in such a way as to allow full freedom to the forces of growth and change. Hence we find Article 21 of the Covenant stating that ' Nothing in the Covenant shall be deemed to affect the validity of international engagements, such as treaties of arbitration or regional understandings like the Monroe doctrine, for securing the maintenance of peace.'

This Article was interpreted by the Assembly as authorizing the conclusion of regional agreements to promote international co-operation or to strengthen the safeguards of peace. The Council was given the right to put the League technical organizations and secretariat at the disposal of member States who wished to hold regional conferences for these purposes. The regional treaties so concluded must of course be in conformity with Article 20 of the Covenant, which declares that ' The Members of the League severally agree that this Covenant is accepted as abrogating all obligations or understandings *inter se* which are inconsistent with the terms thereof, and solemnly undertake that they will not hereafter enter into any engagements inconsistent with the terms thereof.'

The Economic Committee of the League has recommended that the ' most-favoured nation clause ' be interpreted or if necessary revised so as to allow of the conclusion of economic agreements between groups of States for the mutual reduction

of tariffs and other measures designed to remove
the shackles from international trade, provided
such agreements were open to any State that
wished to accede.

There have been a number of regional conferences and committees in the history of the League,
including both members and non-members of the
League and dealing with both economic and political questions.   The European Union Commission
and its various subsidiary bodies is the best known
example.   The Locarno Treaties are the best
known regional agreement for security and the
pacific settlement of disputes based on the
Covenant, but there is a large number and variety
of arbitration, conciliation and non-aggression
treaties, mutual assistance pacts, etc.   The essential features of any League regional agreements are
that (a) they should be closely related to the general
obligations and machinery of the Covenant ; (b)
they should be open to accession by any State that
accepted the conditions of membership.

The Labour Party appreciates the realistic nature
of the Covenant, and is determined to show equal
realism in facing the facts of the present world
situation.   Our aim is, as it has always been, to
make the League world-wide and strong, because
those are the only foundations that can support the
edifice of peace.   In all that we do we shall base
our action four-square on the Covenant.   When
it comes to considering the best methods in present
circumstances we must face the fact that there are
gaps in the League's membership and that a number of countries are in a mood of militant national-

ism. In moving towards our goal of a peace world we shall therefore refuse to be hamstrung by the veto of any nations that may be afflicted by militant nationalism. We will go forward as fast and as far as may be possible with those nations that are willing to co-operate. It is a fact of vast importance that the Covenant gives us a ' constitutional ' basis for a policy of this kind. Present events are proving the wisdom of the statesmen who drew up the constitution of the League in 1919.

It is not possible to predict now what lines this co-operation would follow, nor how many nations would be willing to follow a British lead. It is possible to say, however, that a British lead when given by Labour Governments in 1924 and 1929 has had immense moral power throughout the world. It is also possible to say that as soon as the arms race is checked, rampant nationalism will no longer be an enemy to be feared, and the transition to a peace world will be much shorter and easier than may seem possible to-day. The main purpose of the next Labour Government, therefore, will be to stop the arms race and to put an end to the peril of war, and to secure for this the help of all other nations that genuinely desire these objects. Those who think the price Labour is prepared to pay to deliver us from these evils is too high must propound their alternative.

The British Commonwealth of Nations, if its members act together, will no doubt be able to exercise immense influence in determining whether this policy can succeed. There is no reason to

doubt that the other members will work with the
United Kingdom to this end. ' The Labour Government,' says *For Socialism and Peace*, ' would
regard the Dominions as partners in world leadership for the attack on war ; a wise policy could
secure for our Commonwealth that unity of outlook which is a condition of such leadership.'

The Dominions, like the mother country, are
being drawn into the new arms race. Throughout
the Commonwealth the question of defence is
again uppermost. Hitherto it is the United Kingdom which has borne wellnigh the whole burden
of imperial defence. That imposes on us a corre-
sponding responsibility. It will be the first care of
the Labour Government to explain to the rest of
the Commonwealth just why we consider our
policy of disarmament by international agreement
in exchange for solidly organizing the system of
collective defence on the basis of the Covenant is
the only policy capable of stopping the arms race
and securing the Empire against the danger of war.
Labour is convinced that a full, frank and friendly
discussion with the Dominions on this burning
question will lead to an agreed policy based on
our treaty obligations and on the realities of the
modern world. That policy will put the British
Commonwealth of Nations in the vanguard of
those who are attacking war and laying the foundations of the Peace-World. The peoples of the
Dominions are the same as our people. The
British peoples have never failed to respond to a
bold lead in a worthy cause, or to rally to a policy
which is founded on the rock of common sense

but not afraid to raise the banner of a great ideal.

The Labour Party has always recognized the cardinal importance of co-operation with the United States.   This too is a view that is widespread in the Commonwealth.

The policy of the Roosevelt Administration has been to draw steadily closer to the League, in co-operation through the Disarmament Conference ; for the settlement of disputes (in the Far East and Latin America) ; for international control of the arms traffic (which has been strongly urged by the President and by Mr. Norman Davis at Geneva) ; and for consultation with the Council or Assembly of the League, as to joint action for ending any war or threat of war, on the basis of a non-aggression treaty clarified by an undertaking not to cross frontiers.   The latter offer was made in connexion with a Disarmament Convention, and was coupled with a promise that the President would, by unilateral declaration, undertake that the United States would raise no obstacle to the application of sanctions by the League against a State which the United States concurred in considering an aggressor.

To-day the United States is being drawn into an arms race owing to a direct menace to her safety, at the very moment when American public opinion is exercised over peace.   The phenomenon is so new that the American people are not yet aware of its significance.   But it may be predicted that it will become aware as a result of the naval conversations, and that the question will be asked with more and more insistence, in the United States as in this country—how shall we stop the arms race, which is pushing us towards another world war? The way in which the Soviet Union has reacted to this peril is visible to all men. Who could have foretold two years ago that the Soviet Union would to-day be a permanent member of the Council of the League, and anxious to strengthen the League's collective defence system? If for two years the British Commonwealth gave a bold lead at Geneva on the lines discussed in these pages, who can say what will be the effect on American public opinion, faced by the problem of finding an alternative to the arms race? The Labour Party at any rate is very far from abandoning hope that we may one day welcome the United States in the League of Nations. It is convinced that that day will mark the delivery of the world for ever from the nightmare of war.

Meanwhile let us rejoice that we can count upon the support of the United States for a disarmament plan such as that outlined in Chapter V—the record of the United States at the Disarmament Conference makes that perfectly clear—and on the association of the United States with the Council and Assembly of the League in the latter's attempts to prevent or to stop war. If militant nationalism frustrates our attempts at universal agreement, we can reckon with confidence on the United States co-operating closely with those nations which seek to go forward with the policy described above.

On economic, financial and social questions, too, there is a wide field for co-operation between a Labour Government and the America of the N.R.A. The United States has just become a member of the International Labour Organization and has for years been co-operating in and represented on the economic, financial, health and transit organizations of the League. There are Americans in the Secretariat. Indeed, as regards the technical and humanitarian work of the League America has long been for all practical purposes a member State.

Even before the Soviet Union entered the League the Labour Party spoke of full co-operation with the U.S.S.R. and the latter's membership of any peace and collective defence group as essential. Now that Great Britain and the Soviet Union are both permanent members of the League Council there is a solid basis for the closest economic and political co-operation. Every one of the proposals on disarmament and collective defence adopted by the Labour Party at Southport has been advocated by the Soviet delegation at Geneva. In economic and social policy too, the opportunities for co-operation will be great. On the question of revision of treaties and peaceful change of the *status quo* the Soviet Government see eye to eye with the Labour Party. That is because they share the view that the effective organization of peace and the elimination of the causes of war require a change in the social and economic foundations of society and in the prerogatives of sovereignty. Finally, it must not be forgotten that, whatever may be their views on the proper methods of governing their own country, the international outlook of the rulers of the Soviet Union is based on the fundamental belief of all Socialists everywhere that the ultimate guarantee of peace must be the drawing together of the nations of the world into one Commonwealth, and that this can come about only through Socialism.

Let it be repeated once more, lest misunder-standing arise, that the Labour Government will seek to secure universal agreement on all the proposals which it will make for disarmament, collective defence, joint economic and social policies, common duties of citizenship on the issue of preserving peace, and common dedication to the great aim of establishing a World Common-wealth.

If it is impossible in the first instance to secure universal acceptance for all these policies, it will nevertheless seek to press on with them as far as possible and to secure such actual results as are realizable in co-operation with other nations who will take similar action. All this action will be based solidly on the Covenant and within the framework of the League. But it is not too much to hope that such a policy, when it gave practical results, will exercise a great attractive power for nations which at first may stand aside, for it will become increasingly clear to such nations that a policy of exclusive military nationalism does not confer great benefits upon the nations which pursue it. We can confidently expect that this policy will not be sterile of practical results, and that many, if not nearly all nations will agree readily to co-operate. For there are many nations which to-day are ready to accept :

(a) a wide measure of agreement on the economic, financial and social policies outlined in Chapter IV ;

(b) in some form the idea of a World Commonwealth supported by a world peace loyalty. What this means is explained in the next chapter. In the case of democratic countries acceptance of these two ideals would have to be reflected in some form of Peace Act of Parliament ;

(c) the entire renunciation of war, peaceful settlement of all disputes, and pooled defence programme of Chapter V, together with a standing offer to carry out the whole disarmament plan therein specified, so soon as universal agreement was attainable, and an immediate start with as much of that plan as could be carried out even without universal agreement. Just how far the matter could be carried at the moment would depend on all the circumstances, including the number and strength of the nations who agreed to co-operate, and the armaments and attitudes of the States that preferred to stay outside. The absolute renunciation of war and the categorical undertaking to settle all disputes peacefully and to pool defences could be made effective by the co-operating Governments giving instructions to their Admiralties, General

Staffs and Air Ministries to scrap all plans based on the assumption of the necessity for defence against any one of their number, and to prepare joint plans for the collective defence of all of them against resort to violence against any one of them by an outside State, as tested by the obligations and procedure laid down in the Covenant and in a non-aggression treaty with a definition of aggression. The co-operating nations would also undertake to enforce Article 16 of the Covenant loyally and effectively in all cases to the extent permitted by the collective level of their armaments and their respective geographical positions.

The British Commonwealth has long ceased to prepare against the contingency of attack from the United States. It is the Labour Party's belief that we should similarly dismiss from our minds and from our defence plans the contingency of attack from other States with whom war should be regarded as unthinkable, for example : France, Belgium, Holland, the Scandinavian countries and the Soviet Union, and that we should, on the contrary, endeavour to draw these countries into close co-operation on the lines sketched above. The United States would be on terms of close co-operation with these nations, who would no doubt work out the co-ordination of their foreign policies, as members of the British Commonwealth, the Little Entente and the Scandinavian countries have already done.

The above, it must be repeated, is merely a rough sketch of the lines on which the policy may be developed. How this policy will develop can only be seen when the Labour Government comes to power and begins its efforts to stop the arms race and to remove the danger of war.

The general idea of a foreign policy on these lines is advocated far outside the ranks of the Labour Party. In this country it has been supported by, e.g., Lord Howard of Penrith, Mr. Wickham Steed, Professor Zimmern and others, and has been given the qualified support of *The Times*.[1] It is being strongly urged in France and the Soviet Union, and has supporters in all the democratic countries in Europe and in the United States.

In one way or another the arms race must be stopped and the work of organizing peace must press on victoriously. We must be steadfast in our purpose and realistically adaptable in our methods. In so far as nationalistic resistances and reluctances prevent some States co-operating with us at the outset, we must go ahead without them, though always urging them to join and never resting until we have secured universal agreement. With a dynamic policy on these lines Great Britain could give a lead at Geneva that would transform the League and the world in a few years.

[1] See the leader in *The Times* of October 4, 1934.

Section III

LABOUR'S NEW LEAD

CHAPTER IX

THE INDIVIDUAL AND THE COMMUNITY

THE Labour Party, it will be observed, has come a long way in the search for peace, under the spur of the arms race and of the growing danger of war. It has faced the fact that to organize a universal and enduring peace we must build up a system of world government and that this means drastic changes in the social and economic foundations of the State and in the sovereignty of the State. But once we come so far we must go further : if the organization of peace is to become a reality strong enough to withstand the stress of the anarchic forces making for war, it must mould the laws that bind us all, government and private citizens alike, and must penetrate beyond the laws into the intimate loyalties of the individual.

World government can exist only if there is some direct relationship between it and the citizens in the communities over which its jurisdiction extends. It must have some direct claim on the loyalty of the private citizen and that claim must be publicly acknowledged in the law of the land. Our country, through its membership of the League, is an integral part of an organized community of nations pledged to certain common duties as regards the preservation of peace. Labour contends that it has consequently become the moral and political duty of all good citizens to regard the Covenant of the League as a world constitution which is a prolongation of our national constitution. The Covenant, we hold, is binding not only on the Government but on the Opposition and on every individual citizen. We are all of us responsible for the way in which our country discharges the duties it has assumed, as a member of the League, with regard to the preservation of peace. For, in virtue of our country's membership of the League, we are in some sort world citizens who owe a direct loyalty to the League on the issue of preserving peace that comes before any other public duty. We are not only members of our town, our county, our nation, or even of the British Commonwealth of Nations, but also citizens in the world-wide League of Nations which, in Labour's view, is the beginning of a Co-operative World Commonwealth.

The Labour Government will give effect to this new conception of citizenship by passing a Peace Act of Parliament. This Act will put on the Statute Book our national interpretation of our international obligations : as a member of the League and signatory of the Pact of Paris, Great Britain has solemnly pledged herself not to resort to violence, to submit all her disputes to pacific procedure, and to take joint action with all the members of the League against any

State that perpetrates the international crime of war.

But the treaty obligations of the collective peace system are so novel, far-reaching and unfamiliar, they represent such a complete break with the conditions and traditions of international anarchy, that not only public opinion but politicians and the Press still often speak and even act in perfect good faith in ways which are incompatible with our pledges. There is uncertainty at home as to what our peace commitments mean and doubt abroad as to whether we will, in fact, when it comes to the pinch, act on these new obligations.

The real restraining power of any law lies in the general belief that it will be observed. Great Britain can do more than any other country to create the belief throughout the world that the collective defence system of the League is the only way to break the vicious circle of the arms race and to remove the danger of war. We must find some means of making clear to public opinion here and abroad just how we understand our obligations under the collective system, and equally clear that we are determined to make those obligations the corner stone of British world policy, to act on them without fear or favour in all circumstances.

Therefore, the Labour Government will pass a Peace Act of Parliament in which it will be declared that whereas our country is a member of a world-wide community of nations, pledged by solemn treaty obligations to keep the peace by refraining from war or aggression, submitting all disputes to pacific procedure, and severing all relations with a State that resorts to violence in defiance of these obligations, the British Government shall be bound by this Act :

(1) To submit any dispute with any State to one of the methods of peaceful settlement prescribed in the treaties to which we are a party, and never to resort to force in contravention of those treaties ;

(2) In case the Government felt constrained to resort to force in self-defence, it should immediately report its action and the situation out of which it arose to the League, and shall abide on the basis of reciprocity by any injunctions of the Council or Assembly as to the measures to be taken to restore peace and normal relations ;

(3) It shall have full powers to take all the economic, financial and other measures required to enable it immediately to fulfil, in conjunction with other members of the League, the obligation of Article 16 of the Covenant to sever all relations with a State that has resorted to war in disregard of its pledges to keep the peace.

National legislation on the lines of the Peace Act will help to bring home to public opinion the meaning and importance of our international obligations, and set an example which we should urge other countries to follow. But it is necessary to go further and to face the fact that we cannot make the collective peace system a reality unless we bring about profound changes in traditional views as to the rights of the State over the individual in war time, the duties of citizenship, and the nature of patriotism. So long as the real belief of politicians and the man in the street is that patriotism means ' my government right or wrong,' all pacts and treaties will be mere scraps of paper. In the conditions of international anarchy the natural and spontaneous feeling of love of country was worked up into a blind and exclusive fanaticism, for citizens were taught that their supreme duty was to obey the government whatever happened, even on the life and death issue of war. In England and America, it is true, an exception was allowed on religious grounds for conscientious objectors. But so long as there was no higher political authority than the State there could be no duty of citizenship which could call for the use of private judgement by the citizen as to whether or not the government were justified in resorting to war. It was the duty of citizens, on the contrary, blindly to submit even to being conscripted.

The existence of the League and our membership of the League, Labour claims, has transformed the situation. Specifically it means that loyalty to the world community on the issue of peace overrides any national duty and notably our duty to the Government in war. It can no longer be postulated that citizens owe a blind and unquestioned allegiance to their Government

on the issue of war—' theirs not to reason
why—theirs but to do and die.' It is the duty
of citizens, in virtue of their direct world peace
loyalty, to judge for themselves in the light of
the nation's peace undertakings and obligations,
whether or not the Government has been faithful
on this supreme issue to the overriding world
authority of the League.

Our world citizenship is strictly limited in
nature owing to the limited character of the
treaty obligations that bind us to the rest of
the world community. Therefore, our world
peace loyalty comprises only three duties of
citizenship. But these duties rank first of all
the duties of good citizens. They are :

   (a) Arbitration-insistence—the duty to insist
       that our Government settle all its disputes
       by peaceful means and eschew force ;
   (b) Sanctions-assistance—the duty unflinchingly
       to support our Government in all the risks
       and consequences of fulfilling its duty to
       take part in collective action against a
       peace-breaker with the sole object of
       restoring the rule of international law ;
   (c) War-resistance—the refusal to accept our
       Government's unsupported claim to be
       using force in self-defence ; insistence on
       submitting this claim to the judgement of
       the world community or to the test of
       willingness to arbitrate ; refusal to serve or
       support the Government in any way, either
       by military service or work of national

importance, or the payment of taxes, if it were ever condemned as an aggressor by the League, or designated itself as an aggressor by becoming involved in war after refusing arbitration.

These are the duties which Labour considers are already binding on all citizens in virtue of our country's membership of the League. There is scarcely likely to be any controversy about the first two duties. As regards the third, it may be pointed out that Labour's position had been previously adopted in principle by the League of Nations Union, which has declared that it is its duty to refuse to countenance any war undertaken in disregard of the Covenant. In 1930 the Lambeth Church Conference declared : ' When nations have solemnly pledged themselves by treaty, covenant and pact to the pacific settlement of international disputes, the Conference holds that the Christian Church in every nation should refuse to countenance any war in regard to which the government of its own country has not declared its willingness to submit the matter in dispute to arbitration or conciliation.'

The Labour Party has simply drawn the logical conclusions from principles the justice of which, it will be seen, is admitted far outside its ranks. Labour believes that the responsibility for stopping war ought not to be placed upon the Trade Union Movement alone. Every citizen who wants peace and every other section of the Labour Movement must share the respon-

sibility of any organized action that might be
taken to prevent or stop war, in pursuance of
the three duties of world citizenship by which
the people of this country are bound. Labour is
fully cognizant of the various implications of the
general strike against war. In order to give
the lead to the organized workers and to all
other citizens as to how the three peace duties
enumerated above are to be applied in case
of an emergency, the present Standing Order
VIII (h) of the Trades Union Congress states
that a special congress is to be called in the
event of there being a danger of an outbreak
of war.[1]

The immediate task to which the Labour
Movement will devote itself is to make the meaning
and vital importance of the three world peace
duties, and of the world peace loyalty from which
they spring, understood and accepted by the
public opinion of this country and particularly
by the organized workers. This will give the
maximum guarantee that any government will
observe its League obligations in spirit and in
letter, and will make highly improbable the
occurrence of a situation in which a British
Government would be tempted to resort to war
in defiance of its pledges to keep the peace. But

---

[1] This Standing Order reads as follows : ' In order
that the Trade Union Movement may do everything
which lies in its power to prevent future wars, the General
Council shall, in the event of there being a danger of an
outbreak of war, call a special congress to decide on
industrial action, such congress to be called, if possible,
before war is declared.'

lest any government should ever be tempted to
do so, it is necessary to make it perfectly clear
that the Labour Movement is determined that
Great Britain's pledge to renounce war as an
instrument of national policy shall be honoured
to the full, and that if any government should
ever seek, in violation of that pledge, to involve
Great Britain in war, it will be opposed by the
united strength of the whole Labour Movement
with all its resources.

At first glance these are startling, even revolutionary doctrines. But on closer examination it
will be found that these doctrines are implicit
in the Anglo-Saxon political tradition, in the
humanist and democratic view of the State and
of its relation to the individual that is common
to the English-speaking peoples. Those peoples
have always believed in the welfare State, not the
power State ; they hold that the State must be
the servant and not the master of the people ;
for the State exists for the people and has
been set up by them to serve their common
good.

In order to show how closely the Labour
Party's doctrine of a world peace loyalty follows
the democratic tradition, it may be recalled that
more than half a century ago Thomas Hill Green,
Professor of Moral Philosophy in the University
of Oxford, in a series of lectures on the principles
of political obligation which are recognized as a
classic, advanced the following propositions under
the general title : ' The Right of the State over
the Individual in War ' :

(1) The State derives its right to existence from the extent to which it serves the common good of the people within its jurisdiction. Its purpose should be to realize full equality of rights and opportunities between all its citizens. A State containing privileged classes, or bodies of people thwarted in their development, is imperfect, and its imperfection is a source of danger to other States, giving rise to frictions that might lead to war.[1]

This doctrine is the doctrine of Labour to-day, except that we apply it to the threat to equality that has arisen from the development of the private profit-making system of production, which, as shown in the first part of this book, is leading to combines and monopolies within the State that aggravate the division of the community into rich and poor and breed social injustice at home and a scramble for markets abroad that between them imperil peace. The principle enunciated by Thomas Hill Green and applied in terms of political democracy to the conditions of his time is the very principle that Socialists wish to apply to-day in terms of economic and social democracy to the conditions of the modern world.

(2) War is always wrong, unnecessary and

[1] cf. the statement in the Constitution of the International Labour Organization that social justice is the necessary basis of peace.

harmful, although all the States engaged in war may not be equally responsible. In case of any war the question to ask always is—Who is responsible?

To-day practically every civilized country is bound by treaties which constitute war an international crime and make it a duty of the international community in every case to ascertain who is responsible, and to take appropriate action to put an end to the breach of the peace.

(3) Finally, Green taught that a State is not justified 'in doing whatever its interests seem to require, irrespectively of the effects on other men. If those effects are bad . . . there is no ultimate justification for the political action that gives rise to them. The question can only be . . . where in particular the blame lies.' The State responsible for the wrong, a State that is 'which needs to defend its interest by action injurious to those outside it . . . by no means justifies its purpose and might perhaps be swept away and superseded by another with advantage to the ends for which the true State exists.'

All the Labour Party has done is to apply this last doctrine to this country's membership of a world community, pledged not only to renounce but to prevent and to stop war, which is regarded as the supreme injury a State can commit against those outside it.

That is why Labour holds that it is the international anarchists who are insurrectionary, for they wish to disregard the Covenant, and that is tantamount to breaking the Constitution. The Labour Party takes its stand on loyalty to the Constitution, which now includes the Covenant of the League of Nations of which we are a member.

All that the Labour Party has done is to apply unflinchingly to modern realities and necessities, and particularly to the reality of our membership of the League and to the necessity to put an end to war, the traditional democratic and constitutional doctrines of the English-speaking peoples.

In certain quarters Labour's pledge of uncompromising loyalty to the Covenant and peace has been attacked as calculated to destroy patriotism. But here, too, the Labour Party is being faithful to the best traditions of democracy in the English-speaking countries.

‘ It is utterly false to speak as if the desire for one's own nation to show more military strength than others were the only or the right form of patriotism,’ said T. H. Green, more than half a century ago. ‘ Those who from time to time talk of the need of a great war to bring unselfish impulses into play give us reason to suspect that they are too selfish themselves to recognize the unselfish activity that is going on all round them. . . . Patriotism, in that special military sense in which it is distinguished from public spirit, is not the temper of the citizen dealing with fellow-citizens, or with men who are themselves citizens in their several States, but that of the follower of the feudal chief, or of the member of a privileged class conscious of a power, resting ultimately on force, over an inferior population, or of a nation holding empire over other nations.'

True patriotism, he tells us, is a ' localized or nationalized ' love of mankind, and ' those in whom it is strongest are every day expressing it in good works which benefit their fellow-citizens without interfering with the men of other nations.' He adds that, as a result of the increasing inter-dependence of nations, ' there is no reason why . . . an idea of justice, as a relation which should subsist between all mankind as well as between members of the same State, may not come to act on men's minds as independently of all calculation of their several interests as does the idea which regulates the conduct of the good citizen.'

That is the noblest form of patriotism—through love of and pride in our country we come to love our fellow-men and to love justice. It is because of our patriotism that we Socialists believe our country must give the world an example in loyalty to its plighted word and must base its policy on faith in international justice and in our mission to lead mankind towards a new and fairer civilization in which there shall be neither poverty, tyranny, nor war.

CHAPTER X

TOWARDS A WORLD COMMONWEALTH

THE Labour Party rejects utterly and for ever the maintenance of the Balance of Power as the aim of British foreign policy, and substitutes as its final objective the establishment of a Co-operative World Commonwealth. That, we hold, is a fundamental change in the whole purpose and spirit of foreign policy that results from the lessons of the world war, our membership of the League of Nations, and the menace of the new arms race.

There is a very general admission that the Labour Party is right in putting forward a World Commonwealth as its grand objective. Thus, *The Times* of October 4, 1934, writes : ' It is the prerogative of Oppositions to deal in ideals, and no one will object on principle to the establishment of a " World State " . . . or of the " Co-operative World Commonwealth," which Mr. Henderson proclaimed as the " final aim " of the Labour Party. It is the professed aim, not of one particular party or of one particular Government, but of every country which belongs to the League of Nations.'

On December 13, 1933, in the course of a debate in the House of Commons on the idea of an International Police Force, the case was put from the Labour benches for working towards a World Commonwealth as the basis of British foreign policy. In reply, Viscount Cranborne, one of the younger members of the Conservative Party, said that:

'No one who has considered the subject can deny that the world is becoming internationalized and that it is being welded closer and closer together. If we go a long way back in history, we find that this country of England was originally seven little kingdoms. In time they were combined into one kingdom, with one force to maintain law and order. Later there were added the countries of Scotland and Wales, and if we pass further on we find that these three became one unit in a vast confederation of the British Empire. Nor is there any reason to suppose that that process, which has been going on throughout history, is going to stop now. On the contrary, the increasing communications of various kinds are going to accelerate the process and, perhaps sooner than we imagine, all nations may become parts of one vast world confederation.'

Lord Eustace Percy, also of the Conservative Party, said that:

'My idea . . . is that there is a moral appeal which you are neglecting to make. If you return to the old idea of a great co-operative

H

commonwealth of nations, with great administrative and not merely debating duties for
the securing of a peaceful international order,
and if you apply that idea to the desperate
state of unemployment of Europe and America,
a problem which cannot be solved by any of
your old national or international policies, if you
focus the attention of the nations on that, and
restate international policy in those terms, you
may then indeed give a lead to Europe which
will heal and settle, restore and guarantee peace
in a way that none of your international sabre-
rattling can ever do.'

The difference between Labour and its
opponents is that the latter consider this aim so
remote as to have no bearing on British foreign
policy to-day. They pay tribute to the ' ideal,'
but regard it as irrelevant to the ' facts,' and
attempt to treat the latter by what are virtually
the methods of the Balance of Power. We
Socialists do not believe in keeping ideals and
facts in watertight compartments. We derive our
ideal from a realistic analysis of the facts, and
the existence of our ideal is itself a tremendous
fact which will shape the course of world events.
A profound student of human society, the late
Graham Wallas, once wrote : ' The consciousness
of a common purpose in mankind, or even the
acknowledgement that such a common purpose
is possible, would alter the face of world politics
at once.' That is indisputably true, for ideas
are themselves social facts. Those who believe

that untrammelled sovereignty is indispensable and war ultimately inevitable will, by acting long enough on their belief, stultify the League, push the world back into the Balance of Power and a new race in armaments, and in the end get war. We have gone some way along that disastrous path already.

The only way to stop the new arms race is to practise the kind of foreign policy indicated in the pages of this book. Labour's policy takes full account of two hard facts—the increasing interdependence of nations and the growing deadliness of war; to-day, war anywhere may become war everywhere, and the price of victory and the penalty of defeat alike may be social dissolution and the collapse of civilization. Labour's policy, both on its economic and its political side, has been consistently worked out with reference to modern realities, including our membership of the League. On the other hand, precisely because it is a policy solidly grounded in facts, necessities, and treaty obligations, it is also a policy directed to the establishment of a World Commonwealth as its final objective. Labour insists that current problems can only be satisfactorily solved and immediate decisions and short-term measures can only be effectively taken within the framework of that long-term world policy, which springs from the fundamentals of the Socialist faith and is grounded in the Socialist view of the post-war world.

All who read this book should ask themselves two questions : If the arms race goes on, will it not end in a few years in another war ? Will not another war burn our cities and destroy our people by aerial bombs, gas, and starvation ? No honest man or woman who knows the facts can fail to answer ' yes ' to both those questions.

Many years of work in the cause of peace, culminating in two and a quarter years as Foreign Secretary and three years as President of the Disarmament Conference, have convinced me that the policy set forth in these pages would break the vicious circle of the new arms race and deliver the world from the fear of war that is already dominating public life and poisoning international relations. I do not believe that anything less than this policy would suffice.

Labour's policy is not a policy of half measures. It is a policy of heroic measures ; it involves great risks and heavy sacrifices. But the drift to world war that set in towards the end of 1931 has by now acquired such momentum that it can be stemmed and turned only by a tremendous drive for peace.

The forces making for war are so powerful and so deep-seated in the present structure of society, that there are many who despair and say war is inevitable. But the longing for peace and horror of war are so great in this country and in other countries, that they can overcome all obstacles, however formidable. Labour faces the fact that those obstacles are indeed formidable.

There is a technical side to the business of organizing peace, requiring realistic insight into the forces that move the modern world, expert knowledge, administrative and diplomatic ability, capacity to handle men and affairs. The peace record of two Labour Governments, the foreign policy adopted at Southport and the understanding of the principles of international affairs revealed in the debates on that policy show that the Party can face that aspect of its task with confidence.

The importance of this book lies in the fact that it is a political document, for it sets forth the declared policy of the alternative Government. That policy will stand every test applied by realists and experts in foreign affairs.

But the roots of war lie deep in the private profit-making system of production. A Government that is to make peace must be strong enough to grasp and hold the keys to economic power. It must have the whip-hand over the arms industry and the banks, and must control the whole economic life of the country and base it on the common good instead of private profit as the dominant motive. Those who do not face the necessity for breaking the vested interests that blindly push Governments into war in their scramble for profits are only playing with the problem of peace.

But deeper even than the structure of society is the state of mind that accepts that structure, and with it war, as inevitable. A capitalist society is a fatalist society. Those who believe that the present economic order cannot be changed also believe that national sovereignty is an immutable fact, and that the ideal of a warless and classless world community is but a dream. They only dimly grasp what the Constitution of the International Labour Organization means when it declares that world peace can be secure only if based on social justice, and why the Covenant of the League condemns the private manufacture of arms as an evil.

To make peace, it is essential but not enough to have a big and bold foreign policy. That foreign policy must have as its complement a home policy determined to transform the present social order, and both must spring from a burning faith, the kind of faith that moves mountains. In the last analysis, a foreign policy heroic and clear-sighted enough to put an end to war must issue from a crusade for peace, from a passionate and nation-wide determination to break away for ever from the old world of poverty, anxiety and strife.

To-day, the world is in transition. The vast upheaval of the world war set in motion forces that will either destroy civilization or raise mankind to undreamed of heights. We must go forward to world union or plunge back into anarchy. In that tremendous struggle we Socialists have irrevocably taken sides. It is our faith that it is we who are destined to build the new order on the ruins of the old, to put an end to the economic anarchy and the international anarchy that breed want and war, and to lay the foundations of a broader an d fairer civilization.

To-day the outlook is dark; the forces of reaction are powerful. But we believe that through the Labour Party Socialism can give the world a new lead. Because we love our country and are proud of its great traditions, we will never worship the hateful false gods of nationalism. Our international faith is the soul of our Socialism. That is why Socialism is the only force in the world strong enough and determined enough to break the powers of darkness and reaction and to win through to peace and the brotherhood of man. We summon the youth of this country and the youth of the world to rally to our banner and to press forward with us in this high enterprise, the supreme adventure of all history, the endeavour to bring into being the great Federation of the World as the visible embodiment of the Brotherhood of Man.

THE Covenant binds members of the League to submit any dispute likely to lead to a rupture either to arbitration or judicial settlement, if both parties agree, or to inquiry and report by the Council, at the request of either party, and in no circumstances to resort to war while the dispute is under consideration (a period not exceeding six months in the case of the Council, or a 'reasonable time' in case of arbitration or judicial settlement), nor for three months thereafter. Members of the League are further pledged to accept an arbitral or judicial award, and promise not to make war against a State which accepts such an award. Finally, they are pledged not to go to war against a State that accepts a report of the Council concurred in by all its members except the parties.

A party may refer the dispute from the Council, which consists of fifteen States, including all the great powers in the League as permanent members and a contingent of smaller States elected for periods of three years by the Assembly, to the general conference of the League, in which all the members are represented on an equal footing and which is known as the Assembly. In this case the Assembly acquires all the rights and powers of the Council, except

that an Assembly report, to rank as ' unanimous '
(excluding the votes of the parties), requires only
the votes of the States represented on the Council
plus a majority of the other members of the
Assembly. But if the Council fails to make
a unanimous report the members of the League
recover their freedom of action after three
months. Such a situation has never yet arisen
in the history of the League, but theoretically
there is here a ' gap ' in the Covenant through
which a war might become legitimate.

Since then the great development in arbitration
and the compulsory jurisdiction of the Court
(see Appendix II) on the initiative of the second
Labour Government, have narrowed the ' gap '
by lessening the chance that a dispute would
remain unsettled. The Kellogg-Briand Pact of
1928 (see Appendix V) has deprived its signatories
(including practically all the members of the
League) of the right to fight except in self-defence,
and the Covenant makes it necessary to submit
the plea of self-defence to the judgement (and
action) of the whole League. The second
Labour Government launched a proposal at
Geneva, which the next Labour Government
is pledged to carry out, to revise the Covenant,
so as to make the renunciation of war complete,
and to back it by the obligation, binding on all
members of the League, to put an end to any
breach of the peace.

It is already wellnigh impossible for a State
to resort to war without violating solemn treaty
obligations. Experience has shown three things :

(1) Great Britain is in such a decisive position at Geneva that the presence or absence of a strong British lead generally makes the difference between the League's success or failure.

(2) If no great power wishes to take the risk of applying its treaty obligations the League will fail to act, even against a State it has condemned as an aggressor.

(3) On the other hand, the great majority of the member States, through fear for their own safety if they created a precedent by allowing the League to condone aggression, will insist upon the League making it perfectly clear who is the aggressor and treaty-breaker, and condemning him in no uncertain terms.

These are the lessons to be drawn from the forty odd disputes settled by the League (not counting the Court), including seven that were held to endanger peace and three where hostilities had actually begun. The same conclusions hold good for the League's one failure—the Sino-Japanese conflict.

APPENDIX II

THE setting up of a real International Court, with a small permanent staff of judges and rendering verdicts on the basis of law, had been desired and attempted ever since the Hague Peace Conferences of 1899 and 1907, but became possible only thanks to the establishment of the League of Nations.

The Permanent Court of International Justice at the Hague was set up and is maintained by the League, but is as independent of the Assembly or Council in its verdicts and opinions as British or American Courts are of the political organs of government.

According to the Statute or Constitution of the Court a dispute can be brought before it only if both parties agree. But Article 36 of the Statute—known as the Optional Clause because accession to it is not obligatory on signatories—recognizes the compulsory jurisdiction of the Court, that is, the right of either party to bring a dispute before the Court concerning treaty interpretation ; any question of International Law ; the existence of any fact which, if established, would constitute a breach of an international obligation, and the extent and nature of the damages for such breach. (Some lawyers contend that practically any dispute can be brought before the Court under one of these headings ; in case of doubt it is the Court itself which decides whether it has jurisdiction.) For some years the Optional Clause was signed by only a few States. But the second Labour Government set the example by inducing the whole British Commonwealth to sign the Optional Clause, with certain reservations ; the Optional Clause has now been accepted by no less than forty-two States, including France, Germany, Great Britain, and Italy.

The second Labour Government also signed the General Act of Arbitration, an instrument providing not only for the compulsory jurisdiction of the Court on all questions where the rights of the parties are in dispute, but also for compulsory arbitration of all disputes not settled by other means. The General Act has now been accepted by twenty-one States.

APPENDIX III

THE Convention to Improve the Means of Preventing War gives the Council of the League power to call upon States between whom hostilities have begun to desist from such hostilities and to withdraw their forces behind lines which the Council is empowered to lay down. It gives the Council the right to prescribe other 'conservatory' measures for preventing war, and it imposes an obligation upon the signatories to accept and carry out such measures.

APPENDIX IV

THE Convention of Financial Assistance is an agreement among the Signatory Powers that, if any one of them should be the victim of aggression, the others will co-operate in providing Government guarantees for the payment of interest upon the loans which it may need to issue to enable it to defend its territory. The Convention lays down the maximum sum which each signatory is called upon to guarantee.

APPENDIX V

THE Kellogg-Briand, or Paris Pact, concluded in August, 1928, on the initiative of the United States, contains the following two Articles :

Article I

The High Contracting Parties ' condemn recourse to war for the solution of international controversies, and renounce it as an instrument of national policy in their relations with one another.'

Article II

The High Contracting Parties further agree ' that the settlement or solution of all disputes or conflicts, of whatever nature or of whatever origin they may be, which may arise among them shall never be sought except by pacific means.'

This treaty provides no machinery even for holding a conference. But it has been invoked

by the League, and has proved useful as a con-
stitutional basis for the association of the United
States with the peace-making activities of the
League.

APPENDIX VI

THE Nine-Power Treaty was concluded at the
Washington Conference of 1922, and formed
the political background to the naval agreements
concluded at that Conference. Secretary of
State Stimson, in a note to the League dated
February 24th, 1932, insisted that the Nine-
Power Treaty crystallized what had been American
foreign policy in the Far East for a quarter of
a century, would continue to be the basis of
American policy, and was an essential element
in any agreement to limit and reduce naval
armaments and to refrain from fortifying
American possessions in the Far East.

In the Nine-Power Treaty the contracting
parties, including all the great powers except
the U.S.S.R., undertook to respect China's
sovereignty, independence, and territorial and
administrative integrity; to provide the fullest
and most unembarrassed opportunity to China
to develop and maintain for herself an effective
and stable Government; to maintain the principle of the ' open door ' (equal opportunities for
trade in China); to refrain from seeking to profit
by conditions in China to obtain special privileges
for their nationals; to consult with each other

in case of any differences of opinion as to the application of the Treaty.

APPENDIX VII

By Article 10 of the Covenant ' The Members of the League undertake to respect and preserve as against external aggression the territorial integrity and existing political independence of all Members of the League. In case of any such aggression or in case of any threat or danger of such aggression the Council shall advise upon the means by which this obligation shall be fulfilled.'

Printed in Great Britain by
Wyman & Sons, Ltd., London. Fakenham and Reading.